You Are
So Much
More Than
You Think

*Discover Your Inner Power,
Love Your Authentic Self*

BEVERLY CRERAN

◆ FriesenPress

One Printers Way
Altona, MB R0G 0B0
Canada

www.friesenpress.com

Copyright © 2023 by Beverly Creran
First Edition — 2023

All rights reserved.

All information, tools and practices that are within the book are expressed and shared as seen through my own personal growth, knowledge, learnings and experience of them.

No part of this publication may be reproduced in any form, or by any means, electronic or mechanical, including photocopying, recording, or any information browsing, storage, or retrieval system, without permission in writing from FriesenPress.

ISBN
978-1-03-917473-3 (Hardcover)
978-1-03-917472-6 (Paperback)
978-1-03-917474-0 (eBook)

1. SELF-HELP, PERSONAL GROWTH

Distributed to the trade by The Ingram Book Company

ACKNOWLEDGEMENTS

Thanks to the universe I have been blessed with many loving people who showed up at just the right time to help, teach, guide, love and encourage me. The awakening of my heart, mind and soul allowed my creativity to then bloom within, which led me to the birthing of my book. For all of these experiences, thank you!

Much love and gratitude to Wonnita MacDonald. Without you, who I am now would not be as it is. You were the spark that ignited me, which then allowed me to continue to fan the fire within, and expand my heart, mind, body and soul. I do believe divine timing was at play when we met, for when the student is ready, the teacher appears! Thank you for sharing your wisdom, your friendship and your loving heart!

Thank you to Lee Harris for connecting me to the "Book Doulas" course. Also, perfect timing. Debra Evans and Kristine Carlson were instrumental in not only giving me the tools and confidence I needed to create my book, but they both did it with such heart. Amazing people! Thank you both!

Much love to my wonderful children, Dana Vergata and Chad Creran, their spouses, Marty and Anna, and my mom Anita O'Donnell for all of your continual love and encouragement you've shared. Warms my heart, thank you. I love you all so much!

Dana, my beautiful daughter, I am SO grateful for you being my "tech" person. The loving support and encouragement you continually shared, mixed with the patience and ease in which you guided me, meant more than you'll ever know. You truly helped make this possible for me. Thank you so much!

To my dear friends and soul sisters, Rachelle Tessier, Bonnie Obirek, Lise Jestadt, Judy Kensick and Elaine Unrau, thank you for holding my hand and my heart so gently when I needed you, and for being my rock when I was crumbling. The continual love and friendship that we share means so much to me and has helped me to rebuild the pieces of my life. Love you all!

MaryAnn Kokan-Nyhof, I truly value and love our blossoming friendship. Thank you for believing in me, always being there, and for offering to, and making my book launch a reality and a success! Your kindness touched my heart, truly!

To all of the many other friends and family who shared their time, love or support along the way with me, thank you so much!

And last, but certainly not least, Friesen Press. What an amazing publishing company! You made my journey into self-publishing move with ease. I learned so much. Each one of you on my team were exceptional in the guidance, creativity and designing expertise you shared. You helped my vision grow into a book that I love and am proud to share with others. Kate, you were the glue that held it all together and you gave me the tools I needed to navigate each stage with confidence. Big hugs to you! Thank you ALL so much!

With a full heart, I send love to each one of you. Thank you all for being a part of my journey and my life!

TABLE OF CONTENTS

CHAPTER 1   The Road Travelled 1

CHAPTER 2   The Inside Truths 9

CHAPTER 3   Discovering Your Inner Power 27

CHAPTER 4   What Was I Thinking? 53

CHAPTER 5   Clearing The View 77

CHAPTER 6   Interlude Choosing From The Heart . . . 105

CHAPTER 7   The Eyes of Illusion 113

CHAPTER 8   People Pleasing 129

CHAPTER 9   Love Yourself … The Rest Will Follow . . 147

CHAPTER 10   The "F" Word 167

CHAPTER 11   Sensing, Seeing and Connecting 185

CHAPTER 12   The Loving Hearts Along the Way . . . 205

CHAPTER 13   The Energy of Joy 215

CHAPTER 14   Finding Peace 223

CHAPTER 15   A Destination with No End 233

Works Cited 243

You Are
So Much
More Than
You Think

Chapter 1
The Road Travelled

INTRODUCTION: MY WHY

The abrupt ending of my marriage several years ago and the downward spiral that ensued illuminated for me some of the biggest life lessons, growth and wisdom that I would come to acquire in life. Not only did this event change my world as I knew it, but it also allowed me the gift of opening my heart and rediscovering myself. I was able to accept and love all of myself and thereby release what no longer served me. It ultimately shifted how I now choose to live my life and how I engage with and view others. At the time, I had no idea that the way my divorce was playing out and the pain and trauma I endured through it was actually a gateway that would lead me on a healing and spiritual journey.

It turns out I had been living my life on autopilot. Who knew? Living unconsciously is not a bad thing. It simply means you are doing life routinely, going through your days without noticing your thoughts, yourself or the energy you embody as a result. In other words, you are not connected to your mind, body or spirit. A good analogy of this would be when you are driving and you arrive at your destination, suddenly realizing that you don't remember how you got there. It almost feels like the car drove itself. Life can feel like that too, where one day seemingly flows into the next, sometimes feeling like a blur.

As I began healing myself, my passion to help other women who find themselves in a similar situation began to bubble inside me. I could feel a longing and desire for them to also feel and know the true beauty of who they are; to know their own worth and create a life of joy and contentment moving forward; to not be defined by or stuck in the aftermath of divorce. Yet, as I began thinking about writing this book, I was reminded to see the bigger picture, that there are indeed many women of all ages and in all different circumstances who feel stuck or lost and don't understand why. We are all as unique as the paths we find ourselves on, and yet the same. How we feel and what we desire in life is very often the same: to feel connected and worthy, both with ourselves and with others; to love and be loved for who we are; and to feel happiness, joy and contentment in our lives.

My intention for writing this book is to use my experience to bring self-awareness to you and to inspire you to see the power you have within yourself to create your best life. You are beautiful, and you are ALWAYS worthy and enough just as you are. The truth is, we really are so much more than we think we are or should be, and by connecting with our mind, body and spirit, we gain clarity, compassion and love for ourselves, which in turn will empower us to become the truest, highest versions of ourselves.

I truly believe that the way in which I experienced my marriage ending—the trauma I endured, the awareness I gained and the lessons I learned—along with the timing of it, was meant to be as it was. It became a doorway to allow me to bring presence, consciousness, forgiveness and love into my life so that I can now share my experience, knowledge and wisdom with you at this time. Now more than ever, the world can feel chaotic, both externally and internally, and the peace, joy and love we long for can be found inside all of us. Our life paths are unique to each of us—how we experience, view and live them is our choice. My hope is that this book sparks something inside of you and is a guiding light as you move on your own life path to awakening your heart, mind, body and spirit.

Wouldn't it be amazing if you could allow yourself to be the love and joy you desire in your life, and then watch that love and joy flourish and expand to positively affect those around you? Imagine the potential!

Happiness truly is an inside job ... it's up to us to embrace it

The Storm Before the Calm

Do I want to be here? This was the question asked to me one spring day in 2016 as I sat at the kitchen table, looking through my mail. He (my then husband) was standing in the doorway of our house on his way out to go for a walk, and did not wait for my response. I distinctly remember gazing at him and feeling totally confused as to what he was asking me. I can now see that it was more of a statement, rather than an actual question. I had no idea what would follow it in the coming days, months and years.

I had been married for thirty-plus years, and in my mind, I thought it would be forever. To me, our life together had always felt solid and loving. We had grown together as we moved through the years, raising our two children. We were blessed with a daughter and a son, both of whom were grown and living on their own and we—*I thought*—were beginning to explore the next phase of our lives that was quickly coming upon us: retirement.

However, after that beautiful summer day sitting at my table, my reality quickly changed as I began to realize that what I had thought was true… wasn't. Life as I knew it suddenly changed before my eyes. Shortly thereafter, I found myself heading for a divorce that I had no idea was even a thought or consideration. I felt the rug slowly being pulled out from under me, leaving me with no legs to stand on. Shock, disbelief, grief and denial ravaged through my body, seemingly mixed as one, and invaded every fibre of my being, leaving me feeling numb, motionless and engulfed in fear. My heart, once filled with love, was now shattered, and I was rocked at the very core of my being. I can only explain it as feeling like I was outside of my body, watching. I could see what was happening and hear the words uttered, but neither could actually penetrate my mind. Nothing made sense to me, and it slowly became a recipe for crazy-making.

My tears were an endless flow of water that began from the inside of my heart and soul and felt like a raging waterfall leaving my eyes. My mind would not stop trying to make sense of it all and became a playground for all the possibilities and stories I could tell myself, which led me to the relentless scenarios of all the would'ves, could'ves and the long list of I should've's. This ultimately led to no rest and ongoing sleepless nights. I felt like I was dreaming and desperately needed to wake up. *HOW WAS THIS HAPPENING?*

While married, I was mainly a stay-at-home wife and mom, working casually or part-time when my kids reached school age. Staying at home was a decision that we had both thought was important for our children and one that I embraced wholeheartedly. I took pride in staying home, loving every step of the way as the years passed. Everything from changing diapers to making it through the teen years, watching them both blossom into the amazing adults they are today was my life, my joy and how I saw myself in the world. It gave me a feeling of worth and purpose. Now, with my entire family seemingly broken. *WHO WAS I?*

Everyone was telling me, "Take care of yourself," and "It's all about you now." It surprised me and quite honestly scared me a little when I began to realize that I had no idea what that meant, how to do that or what I even needed. *WHY WAS THAT?*

When my life suddenly took this turn, it felt like I was standing at a crossroads. Who I was, what I was going to do, where I was going to go and how I would experience it all was unclear and unknown—it was horrifying. It felt like my whole world had collapsed. Everything I'd known and believed had crumbled, and I was left lying within the rubble.

The road I found myself on was in no way easy, fast or straightforward. As I navigated the days, months and years ahead, I was met with many blocks, detours and do-overs. In my mind there seemed to be no blessings or light, only darkness.

In the coming years, I slowly started becoming aware of how and why this happened. When the river of tears subsided, I was able to begin to refocus, love and heal myself and the wounds that I embodied. Wounds that I had no idea had been in me for quite some time were now rising up in me with the grief of my marriage ending. What had started out as extremely dark and painful to me, would in time slowly transform and shift my unconsciousness to conscious awareness and allow my true self to begin to emerge.

My heart, once shattered, is now fully open and I am able to feel and embrace the love and joy both inside of myself and around me. I am grateful for who I am, the people I share my days with and the journey that got me here. I believe wholeheartedly that everything happens when and as it's meant to, and divine timing is always at play. My hope is that you may connect with a part of this book or my story and begin to share the same outlook in your life. You don't have to go through a traumatic event like I did. Simply being willing to allow yourself to stop for a moment and inquire within will bring awareness to the forefront and is the first step. The people you encounter daily and the situations and life events you deem as difficult or hurtful are doorways for opportunity. They are there to show you the aspects of yourself that are in need of healing. The choice is yours to open the door and look inside.

Start over my darling,
Be brave enough to find the life you want
and courageous enough to chase it.
Then start over and love yourself the way you
were always meant to.

MADALYN BECK

Chapter 2
The Inside Truths

FEELING WITHIN

Have you ever noticed that when you hold a newborn baby you can feel an aura of pure love and joy coming from them? Do you ever wonder why? Well, it's because that is who they truly are, and their energy radiates from them so that we can feel it when we hold them. Pure love is at the core of their essence and soul. We are all born beautiful babies, and therefore the same energy is within all of us. In fact, everything is energy. Like us, the plants, animals, material objects and vast space that surrounds us are also all made of the same energy and are part of existence. Why?

Because everything exists. The energy is actually made of tiny particles of expansion, light and harmony—it is made of love. I first learned this in a mindfulness class, and I must say it was something that I had never really thought about, yet I found myself intrigued. I also learned that this high vibration energy is our divine connection to our higher selves. Some call it our God part, but you will hear me reference it as the universe throughout the rest of this book.

This higher energy, although beautiful to feel, is not sustainable as our energy fluctuates throughout our day based on our experiences, and how we choose to respond or act as a result of each experience. The frequency of our energy is what affects how we feel and how we experience our daily life. Low frequency occurs when you feel off, perhaps fearful, sad, angry, anxious or frustrated, and high vibration would feel more loving, calm, light and happy.

Imagine walking into a room where you can immediately feel tension, giving you a good sense of what might be happening there before any words are exchanged. I've heard this referred to as "the air was so thick you could cut it with a knife." That thick air feeling is actually the energy being emitted from the people in the room. This is how we feel the energy of others.

An example of how our own energy creates our days might be seen when you find yourself in low energy—perhaps you are upset, scared or angry. Consider who you gravitate towards when you feel this way. Most people initially might find someone who will share in their frustrations or validate them, and as a result they feed off each other's lower energies. Their exchanged words, although they may be helpful, also keep the low vibrations flowing. Therefore, you continue to feel unhappy, possibly even after the conversation ends. We then have the potential to carry this low negative energy with us throughout our day, for it remains in us until it is cleared.

Alternatively, when we are in high energy, life flows with more ease and we seem to attract and gravitate toward others who feel the same. If we are met with someone who is in lower energy, it might jolt us out of our good feelings as it can be easy at times to get pulled into their world.

Our words, feelings, thoughts and tone in which we express ourselves all carry a frequency or vibration. The words we speak and the thoughts we think create how we will experience our daily life. How we communicate with others and ourselves and the energy associated with the words we choose is felt in our bodies. When you are angry you really don't think to stop and see how your body is feeling, but my guess is it would be tense and contracted. The reason why we don't feel our bodies is because most of us are living our days on autopilot and quite unconsciously. Most of us are simply too busy, consumed with whatever tasks are at hand and just trying to get through the day. We don't take the time to stop and see how we are actually taking it all in. As a result, most days we are totally unaware of any bodily sensations, leaving us disconnected from our inner world. And depending on what occurs during our day, our energy continually fluctuates from low to high and back again, sometimes leaving us falling into bed, exhausted from it all.

Looking back, it was very apparent that during my divorce I was in low vibration pretty much continually, all day, every day. I would simply wake up in the same low energy I went to bed in. It was who I was at the time. It stood to reason that because I felt my world was negative and unhappy, the energy within me and around me would be too. My emotions and feelings were raw and so interchangeable. I could move from anger to grief to denial within moments of each other, and honestly, I sometimes felt all of these simultaneously. Most of all, fear was ravaging through me continually, and growing every day. Fear of the unknown, fear of my future and fear of all the uncertainties associated with my new reality, like being alone now. My body and mind were in constant stress and anxiety, giving them no rest and therefore no peace. I felt paralyzed at times, unable to make any clear decisions, fearing I would make the wrong one. It was all so exhausting, and not at all how I wanted to feel. On top of it all, I felt powerless, as I had no idea how to change how I was feeling.

In a world where we desire and want instant solutions to our problems, I would find out that would not be the case here. I would instead find that I would have to start at the beginning and slowly learn to feel and connect with myself through my energy, mind and body.

Your energy is the road map that leads to awakening your mind, body and spirit

The following simple techniques are ones that I found helpful to begin this process. Some of these are still my go-to practices today when I'm feeling out of balance or scattered. Sensing, feeling and connecting to the energy within your body are the guideposts that will lead you on your journey of self-discovery and self-awareness.

- Rub your fingertips together swiftly for thirty to sixty seconds, then stop and hold your hands at your sides. Can you feel anything? A tingling sensation in your hands or fingertips? Just notice.

- Sit quietly and still. Close your eyes and focus inwards. Begin to notice your breath for a few moments. Then breathe in slowly and deeply through your nose to a count of four, hold for a count of two, then breathe out slowly through your mouth for a count of four. How does your body feel? Is there any tension in your neck, shoulders, back or anywhere else? If so, repeat the breath exercise and with each slow exhale, focus on the tense area and release and relax it a little more. Feel yourself letting go. As you become more aware of your body, can you feel or notice any other sensations? Your heartbeat or pulse? It's OK if you don't, but if you notice something, sit with it for a moment to connect with yourself. There's no right or wrong way to do this, or right or wrong way to feel. Everyone is different, so allow whatever you are feeling, or not, to be as it is. Just bring your awareness to the forefront.

- Hold your right hand out in front of you. Focus on it. In your mind, ask yourself, "How do I know I have a right hand?" Remain focused on your hand and repeat the question if needed. Notice if you can feel any sensations in your hand or fingertips.

It took me a while to feel any sensations with these exercises in the beginning, as I was not able to focus for long periods of time. My mind and my body were both wound pretty tight. However, it did become easier in time, with practice. I would come to understand that this was a journey, not a race—I was not in competition with anyone and there was no deadline to achieve. There was just me, getting to know me.

The key is to take each moment as if it's the first and allow it to be as it is. You may feel connected and feel the sensations or energy one time and find it more challenging the next. This is perfectly OK! Baby steps are what lead us to leaps and bounds!

Aligning with the Energy

Our energy centres, or chakras, are a vital part of our body that affects how we feel within and therefore, also how we show up in the world. There are seven different chakras in the body, and they run parallel along the spine, from the base all the way up to the crown of the head. When they are open and flowing we feel balanced and in alignment with life: we feel a sense of ease, love and joy within us. Alternatively, when they are blocked due to stress, illness or emotional upset, we may instead have feelings of unworthiness, unease or be filled with fear and doubt. I was once told that the chakras are like a hose in the body. If the hose is straight, aligned and free of blockages, water flows freely through it. However, if there is a kink in the hose, the water builds up unable to move, and then becomes stuck. Our energy is the same. Clearing your chakras with meditation or energy work allows your energy to flow freely. As a result, you will feel more balanced, stable, confident and secure in your body and in your mind.

Let's take a closer look at the seven chakras to get a better understanding of what each one is responsible for.

1. The Root Chakra, sometimes called the physical chakra, is at the base of the spine and is a beautiful red colour. This is where our physical well-being, sense of being grounded and stability lie.

2. The Sacral Chakra, sometimes called the emotional chakra, is a couple of inches higher on the spine, just below the belly button. It is a vibrant orange colour. This is where our emotions, feelings, sexuality and creative expression are found.

3. The Solar Plexus, sometimes called the mental chakra, is just above the belly button. It is a glorious sunshine yellow. This is where our wisdom, decision making, personal identity (power and will) and gut feelings come from. It's also where our ego resides.

4. The Heart Chakra is directly by the heart and is surprisingly not red, but a beautiful green colour. It is the centre of love, compassion, empathy and forgiveness. There is also an upper fourth chakra, the Feminine Centre, which is pink in colour. It is located midway between the heart and throat chakras and is the gateway to the last three higher spiritual chakras. Although guided meditations do not usually include the upper fourth as a chakra, I have found that pausing there and allowing yourself to move through the gateway to the higher realms is beneficial.

5. The Throat Chakra is situated in the neck area. It is light blue or turquoise in colour and is responsible for communication and self-expression. When it is open and flowing, you are able to speak your truth easily. It is also where communication and guidance with your guardian angel is possible when focused on through meditation.

6. The Third Eye Chakra is focused between your eyebrows and is a brilliant indigo or purple colour. It is where your intuition, awareness and connection to your higher self lie. When open and connected to it, you may feel a pulsing sensation in the brow area between the eyes.

7. The Crown Chakra is at the top of your head and is a violet or white colour. Spiritual and higher understanding can be attained here. It lifts and inspires you and is your connection to the divine.

There are many beautiful guided chakra meditations available on the internet. These are perfect when you need guidance moving up each one, from your base to your crown, and they also allow you to choose the length of meditation that you think you can achieve in the beginning. I suggest starting with a five-minute one at first, if you are new to meditating. Following a guided meditation is also helpful to focus and quiet your mind, as focusing on the instructor's words and repeating them in your mind can ease your many thoughts.

You can also try to meditate on your own. Start by simply sitting quietly. Begin with the same breath work you would use to connect to your inner energy: close your eyes and focus inwards, connecting to your breath for a few moments. Then take a few deep, slow breaths in and out: breathe in to the count of four, hold for two, and release to the count of four. Take your time as you repeat a few rounds of this breath work. Then, say in your mind, "I hold the intention to open all of my energy centres simultaneously. All of my centres are open and flowing." Continue to sit quietly and become aware of your body in that moment. Can you feel anything? Any pulsing, throbbing or warmth anywhere along your spine? Just notice. It is totally OK if you don't feel anything the first few times. I have found that it can take a while, so please, no self-judgment. Just awareness.

Allowing yourself the time to notice and connect to how you feel is the first step. Quieting the mind will allow space for this to occur more easily. A sense of calm or stillness may be attained by simply sitting quietly and breathing or by meditating. Bringing these two aspects into your day will, in time, allow you to move into more calmness.

Honestly, meditation did not come easily to me and was not something I'd ever thought about doing in past years. I'm not sure I ever would have tried it had I not found myself in the situation I was in. As I began to meditate, I found that my mind felt like it was on a hamster wheel, going round and round, so I also found that patience and practice was needed. I tried my best to take one day at a time. I incorporated meditation into my day regularly, either at home or in classes. At home, I would put ear plugs in and listen to one as I sat on the couch or lay in bed before sleeping. This would, in time, bring a sense of calmness within me and aided in my sleepless nights.

In the beginning stages of learning to meditate, I found it helpful to repeat the words or phrases in my mind along with the teacher. It helped me to stay focused and also stopped the mind clutter (or at least slowed it down slightly). Also, another helpful tip is to not worry about sitting properly. Yes, the pose of sitting cross-legged, palms up and back straight is traditional, however if that's not comfortable or possible for you, then simply sitting in a chair with your legs uncrossed, feet on the ground and palms in your lap, or lying in bed, also works. Your mind will still likely wander no matter what method you choose, and that is totally natural and OK. Simply bring it back to the meditation and refocus either on the guided words or on your breath when you notice you've strayed. There is no right or wrong way to learn meditation. So, if you are trying to begin meditating for yourself, then first of all good for you, and second, remember to be gentle with yourself. You are exactly where you are meant to be. I do believe the universe not only guides us to what we need, but does so when we need it and at a time when we are ready to embrace it.

I can recall one of the first times I did chakra meditations and how I felt unsure of the whole process: the position of sitting, trying to calm my thoughts and wondering how on earth I would ever feel anything in my body. Being in a class felt helpful, as I could sense that maybe others felt the same way too. I began breathing and focusing inside and really connected with the woman teaching. Her voice was so calming and soothing. I first placed my attention on my Root Chakra (physical) and opened it. Then, in my mind, I slid up my spine to the Sacral Chakra (emotional), and as I repeated her words in my mind, "Open, open, open, and allow for optimum flow," I began to feel a single stream of water trickle down my cheek. I remember feeling a little embarrassed that this was happening, yet I continued with the meditation to the end. I was told afterwards that the tears were my body's way of unblocking and releasing the negative stuck energy in my body. It was a positive thing to occur as it meant I was indeed connecting within. The tears did not happen every time I meditated in the coming days, but they allowed me to understand the importance of opening my chakras, and they also were the beginning stages of me feeling connected with myself. As you begin to open your chakras, be willing and allow whatever is needing to shift or clear within you. Clearing your chakras once a week is a small way of giving yourself love, and it benefits your whole being, mind, body and spirit.

The Time Is Now

As you begin to connect to your bodily sensations and energy and bring stillness into your days, you then open the door to become more mindful.

Mindfulness is simply the quality or state of being conscious and aware; taking notice of where you are and using your five senses to connect with that. We all have the ability to use our senses more effectively—to take the time to actually touch, see, hear, smell or taste what is in front of us.

Presence is when you actually feel connected to where you are. Your mind is quiet, and you accept, embrace and enjoy what is happening in the moment. You are there in it. In time, you may find that the things around you seem to become more defined or brighter somehow while in the present moment.

How will you know when you are present? ... When you no longer have to ask.

So, how do you begin to focus, to become more mindful or present? Honestly, I was open to try any and all suggestions that came across my path. Some of the following techniques I still use to this day, while others were simply a good thing in the moment.

- The first thing I started doing was something I heard from the instructor in one of my first mindfulness classes. Her suggestion was that while I was in my car or driving, to say to myself in my mind or out loud, "Right hand on the wheel, left hand on the wheel, I feel the wheel," while physically placing each hand on the steering wheel. Doing this connects your words and sensations as you feel the wheel, and allows you to become present. I found this helpful, so I then began implementing my own versions of this exercise by noticing and feeling the seat under my bottom or noticing and saying to myself, "I'm passing this street," naming it as I drove by. These quick tools easily became my daily practice and are things I continue doing today if I am feeling scattered.

- Randomly stopping during the day to check in on how your body is feeling, and taking a moment to breathe, can slow down any stress you are feeling and bring your body and mind back to calmness. This also helps to bring you back to the present moment. If needed, you can repeat a phrase in your mind, like "breathing in calm, breathing out anxiety," or choose words that best suit your needs at the moment. This practice doesn't change your day, but rather it changes how you feel so you can then choose to move through your day more easily.

- Having a mindful shower is a wonderful thing to give yourself, and it is something I definitely did not do in the past. I would usually get in and out fast, sometimes not even remembering washing my hair. I begin by standing under the falling water, sometimes closing my eyes for a moment as I breathe in and out, allowing myself to connect to how I am feeling, and if needed, reminding myself that everything is OK. Then I feel the warm water bounce off my head and trickle down my face and cheeks, following it down to my shoulders, and then as it runs down my body until it pools at my feet. I smell the soap and feel the bubbles as I wash each part of my body. This is a great way to begin the day.

- I came across a mindful colouring book one day and thought, *Why not?* To my surprise, I found it was not only fun because it brought back a child-like essence, but as I focused on colouring, my mind would slow down, I became more in the moment, more present, and I felt more relaxed.

- Taking a mindful walk in nature can allow you to connect to the beauty that is in everything around you. As you walk, simply stop for a moment, close your eyes and breathe a few deep breaths. When you open your eyes, gaze around, without thought for a few seconds and then take in your surroundings: feel the warmth of the sun or the breeze on your face. Notice the earth beneath your feet and the vastness above you or take a moment to witness nature's beauty. As you begin to do these things more, you will begin to see and feel the connection we all share to all that is.

There are many ways to become more mindful in your day by simply bringing awareness to yourself, your surroundings, your senses and your body, and feeling the associated sensations and energies. A saying I love, and one I use when feeling scattered is to simply say, *"Keep your mind where your body is."* This allows me to stop, refocus and come back to the present.

I would find myself often taking the time to randomly check in with myself during the day. One evening, I was at home sitting on the couch, all cuddled up and warm in my favourite soft, fuzzy blanket. I was watching a movie on tv. It was a comedy, and a funny one at that. You would think that I would be feeling fine as I was relaxing, enjoying the movie. So, it surprised me when all of sudden I became very aware of my body sitting there, and how it felt tense and my shoulders were raised slightly, and not at all feeling relaxed. *What?* I thought, pausing for a minute, now feeling confused. The truth is, we have many subconscious thoughts, and even though they don't all land on us directly, we can still feel the energy of them. I obviously had something going on in the background, so I paused the movie and closed my eyes and took some deep breaths. I concentrated on releasing and lowering my shoulders with each breath and reminded myself of the truth of where I was by saying, "I am OK and safe. I am sitting on my couch. I have everything I need. All is well."

The negative or low energy we embody, whether or not we are aware of it, remains in us until we notice, feel and take steps to release it. Each time we do this, the energy begins to lessen slightly. Awareness of your energy and bodily sensations are guideposts that lead the way in discovering how you feel throughout your day, and it is when you are aware that you can then choose to shift or change yourself, your day and your potential outcomes.

Chapter 3
Discovering Your Inner Power

*The awakening of consciousness
is the evolutionary step for mankind.*

—ECKHART TOLLE

The Flashlight

Gaining conscious awareness is something we all have the power to achieve. It is within each of us. Throughout the years I have heard it defined in several different ways, the following are a few of those definitions:

- It is your noticing ability, your Christ Light.

- Consciousness exists in the space between your thoughts and is the basis of how we create.

- Consciousness is your God-given right to place your focus somewhere or on something. Think of it like a flashlight. Where and what you shine the light on, you will then experience.

Most of us live our days unconsciously, unaware of ourselves and how we are creating our own lives. By bringing more awareness to yourself, your surroundings and your now or present circumstance, you can choose to refocus. This has the potential to shift, change or renew your reality.

We are all the same at our core, and we all create through our thoughts and associated energies, either consciously or unconsciously. Our energy connects us to ourselves, each other and the universe, which we also are connected to and co-create with. Our lives may appear very different on the outside, however, we all feel and create the same on the inside.

How? Remember, everything is energy. What we think, say and how we react to people and situations directly affects how we will experience them and whether we will feel low or high vibrations.

We create in two ways:

- Consciously, by becoming more aware and still, and choosing to place our focus onto something intentionally.

- Unconsciously, by allowing our programming, beliefs, patterns and upbringings to govern us. Unconscious creation happens when we are not present, but instead are living in the past or are overly concerned about the future.

Creating consciously is an ability we all have. We do this by focusing and holding our attention on what we want or desire and setting an intention around it. As an example, you might say, "I intend to bring more joy into my days." You would then take steps to shift your negative thoughts and instead place your focus (consciousness) onto more joyful things, situations or people during your day.

Alternatively, the unconscious programming that is stored in our subconscious may contribute to how we show up in the world, how we feel and why we find ourselves triggered or upset by certain people or situations. Most of us are totally unaware of our programming, why it's there or how it got there. Why? Well, because these are the things that happened to or around us throughout our lives that were negative, painful or hurtful. We tend to choose to push these memories down, to not look at them, eventually believing they have gone. When in fact, we have buried them in our subconscious, and we are simply unaware that the energy of them remains in us. So, what does this mean?

Everything weaves together in time. As you become more mindful, aware of your energy and how your body feels, you can then begin to choose to place your focus (consciousness) onto other things when you feel out of sorts. In other words, when you notice that you feel tight or like your body is contracted, pay attention to what you are focusing on or thinking. In that moment, you have the option to look at it and choose to refocus on something that is happy or loving instead. This will begin to raise your vibration and shift your energy from lower to higher. This process is discussed and referred to throughout the book in various aspects and examples, as it is key to gaining more self-awareness.

I will be honest, this was definitely a long process for me in the beginning. Shifting my focus to something that was happy and loving, when I was feeling anything but that, was not at all easy. I could however, stop, breathe and calm myself, so I learned to take the small successes in each moment. I would later become aware that there are many smaller lessons within each of the big lessons. For me, this smaller one was learning patience and accepting where I was. Everything happens when it is meant to, not necessarily when you want it to or how you think it should.

As time passed, I began to understand that fear was the culprit that kept me feeling stuck and unable to shift. Fear can show up in many forms and in an array of feelings and emotions. Anxiety, frustration, doubt, guilt, shame and anger are all under the umbrella of fear. Each one directly or indirectly affects how you see yourself, your self-worth, and therefore how you show up, both for yourself and with others. When you live in fear of any kind you are limiting your world and your potential in it because you are limiting yourself. When you fear making the wrong decision, you can at times feel frozen, unable to decide anything at all. Each negative fearful thought builds upon the next and as a result, you feel justified in your decision to remain as you are. You may come to believe that you *can't* be, do or attain something, and when *can't* becomes your belief, you simply *won't*.

I love this breakdown of the word fear:

F alse
E vidence
A ppearing
R eal

Fear is a feeling that we allow in our being by focusing on something that's deemed wrong, hurtful or perhaps scary. The energy associated with it covers up, in a sense, our true nature that we are: love. Although love is always there, for the moment or period that we feel fear, we simply cannot feel it. Fear may be helpful to feel in times of danger as it can alert us to pending threats and helps to keep us safe, however, if it's not there for safety reasons, it is not needed and only hinders or suppresses us in some way instead.

The antidote for fear is:

- Becoming conscious.

- Allowing the situation to be as it is.

- Accepting where and who you are.

- Trusting in the universe—knowing that when one door closes, another opens.

Allowing, accepting and trusting are a few key steps in releasing any negative low energy such as fear. Time, patience and dedication may be needed as you move through each step. Yet, when you have attained freedom from fear, you will begin to create from a place of truth and not from old patterns or beliefs.

It's OK to have bad days—we all do. But if one bad day moves into days, or longer and you feel stuck, then try to refocus. Speak truth to it by telling yourself, "OK, I've had a really crappy day or perhaps week, but I'm now going to refocus on something that will change that." For whatever negative feelings that have arisen during your bad day or week are now in the past. Ruminating over them only creates more of the same in the present. So instead, go for a walk, play a game, go out with a friend or hug your kids or grand kids. Place your consciousness on something that will bring a feeling of joy and love into yourself and your day. This doesn't change what happened in the past, but it has the potential to shift or change what will happen in your *now*.

Remember, what we choose to focus on and the words we speak create our experience. The words "*I am*" are powerful for a couple of reasons. In Sanskrit, *so hum* means "I am that." It is a statement of the truth of who you are: your existence, your spirit, your connection to your higher self or the universe. If we use the words "*I am*" when referring to an aspect of ourselves, we are stating that we are a certain way, not only to ourselves, but also to the universe. This works with both positive and negative statements. Saying "I am confident and smart," can bring a sensation of worthiness and give you a can-do attitude so you believe that anything is possible, and you may feel drawn to try new things and, therefore, grow. On the other hand, saying, "I am so stupid," can make you feel like you don't compare to others, and therefore, you may not give yourself the chance to try something new because you fear that you are not capable or deserving of it. Both statements, when repeated over time, can become our beliefs and how we see and view ourselves, and therefore, they can create our life possibilities.

The following was an event that occurred during the same time as the unfolding of my marriage, where this truth and the power of these words were revealed to me:

I was at my lake, in a mobile home we had bought many years prior to the divorce; a place that carries many wonderful memories in my heart of all the laughter, love and music that had been shared together throughout the years. It was a place that when it was time for us to begin to split our assets up, I wasn't really sure why I thought of keeping it. Although I am able to deem all of those memories as wonderful now, back then they haunted me with immense sadness. And yet, somehow, I felt very strongly that keeping the home was the right thing to do.

This one morning, while at the mobile home, I remember opening my eyes and one of the first thoughts in my mind was to go to the beach, which was not something I did routinely. But it felt like I was being drawn or pulled there somehow. So I finished my coffee, got dressed and made my way down the road that leads to the beach. When I arrived, the beach was still deserted as it was quite early, so I sat for a moment on a wooden bench overlooking the sand and water, just gazing out at the vastness of the lake. The sky was bright blue, and seagulls and birds danced above and in front of me. I could feel a sense of calmness and peace rising within me, and recall thinking how incredibly blessed I was to be there. I began taking steps onto the sand and then along the water's edge, feeling the stillness in the air around me. In front of me, laid a bank of rocks that jetted out into the water, and beyond that more sand. Although I was alone, in that moment I felt like I wasn't. I moved over to the other side of the rocks and sat on a big boulder lodged in the ground and could feel the warmth of the sun penetrating my skin. As I sat looking outwardly at the water, the distant waves seemed to come alive to me as each one rolled into the next, and I remember feeling connected somehow, like I was a part of them. As I brought my eyes closer to shore, I closed them for a moment, and when I reopened them, I found the ebb and flow of the waves across the sand also seemed to feel alive to me. I felt this overwhelming sensation that I was connected to each rolling wave that seemed to glisten as it reached the shore. I was in awe of the beauty. I then glanced over a few feet in front of me and saw a big, thick stick in the sand. I walked over and picked it up, and without even thinking began writing big bold letters in the sand: I AM OK. Each letter seemed to permeate my mind and body as it etched in the sand. I stood there for a moment and reread the words a few times to myself in my mind, then out loud.

As I made my way back to my trailer, I felt a sense of ease come over me. I thought that even though my outer world did not echo that feeling, I somehow knew that deep down I truly was OK. Writing the words "I AM" in the sand that day brought with it an inner awareness and a new belief that I could now choose to refocus on and make my reality moving forward.

Something shifted in me that morning, and it strengthened my state of awareness. I believe it was my first real moment of experiencing true presence. In that moment, I was totally there, conscious of myself, my surroundings and connected to the wonders before me. I felt the beautiful connection I share not only with the universe, but also with everything around me. The words written in the sand were a confirmation that I needed to hear, see and feel, and therefore, came through me.

From Discovery to Awareness

It can feel at times like one day flows into the next. There never seems to be enough time to do the things we say we'd love to do, and yet we somehow accept that that's just the way it is. Why is that? Do you ever wonder where our time goes?

In the coming months, after being at my trailer, I was met with more and more feelings of connection, awareness and curiosity. Each day, I became a little more aware of where and what I was focusing on, both consciously and unconsciously. I knew there was still a lot of negative chatter and energy going on, both in me and around me, but I didn't yet know what exactly it was about or why it happened, so I began looking at a few things a little more closely. I became curious about how I was spending my time and how that impacted what I was creating in my life. So, I took some mental notes on myself for a while, regarding the following things:

- My phone: What did I look at while on it? How much time did I spend on it?

- My surroundings: Negative situations or people—whether I was actually with them, involved in them, or focusing on them in my mind (ruminating)

- My time: What did my days entail? How was I choosing to spend my time?

- My unconscious tendencies: What was I unconsciously allowing into or pushing away from my life?

  My happiness: What brought a smile to my face? What didn't?

- My desires: What did I really want more of in my life? Was I creating it?

Discovering the answers to these questions would allow me to then decide what I could shift or change in my days.

Gaining awareness of what I actually had control over and what I didn't allowed me to then make conscious decisions to shift and refocus myself and my actions to bring more joy, peace and love into my days.

Creating Online Balance

Technology and social media are both instrumental in our daily lives. It's how we connect with each other, both personally and through our work, how we now often shop and it also allows us to connect to people around the world, which, when you think about it, is unbelievable! In many ways it can and does make our lives better, easier and less complex, which is what we all crave and long for, right? But is it creating ease? Is it really all good? And what does too much screen time take the place of in your days? Everyone says they want more balance and less stress. They say they never have enough hours in their day to do everything, yet never stop to look at why.

In order to shift or change something in our lives, we first have to become aware of what we are actually doing in them. As I mentioned, there was a time when I took notes on my phone habits, and I was surprised by the results of how much time I actually indulged and how it all affected me. Although, it was by this awareness that I was then able to choose the best way to proceed moving forward to shift my focus and create more balance within myself and my life. I also began to notice that as you gain self-awareness, you also become aware of others too. I think it's a fair statement to acknowledge that a lot of people have become somewhat addicted to technology in one way or another: perhaps by engaging with TikTok, Facebook and Instagram; by playing games with infinite levels; by searching Google endlessly for no real reasons; or maybe by a combination of them all. Some people put their entire lives on their phones and therefore believe they are lost without them. But why? What drives that feeling or urge to do this? Has it somehow become a part of how we validate ourselves to the world?

Have you ever thought about what would happen if you chose to be more present? To really experience where you are in the moment? How would this affect your days? Could you consider disconnecting slightly or setting limits on screen time? If so, what does that thought bring up in you? How would you feel doing so?

Social media in particular has become so easy to participate in that we just do it naturally and without any thought sometimes. We are simply unaware that underneath the fun of it, we may be unconsciously seeking some sort of validation, acceptance or love from the reactions and responses to our posts. The more positive reactions we get, the more we want. By wanting this, we are looking outside of ourselves to make ourselves feel good. It's like a drug, and we are creating beliefs around why we need, want or have to have it. Technology is awesome, you believe, but what happens when reactions are negative or you don't receive many "likes," or someone doesn't respond the way you think they "should"? Do you get triggered or upset? And if so, by what? How do you feel? Our responses to and how we engage with social media are so automatic and ingrained in our daily lives that we don't stop to feel anything. We are simply running on autopilot, following the status quo, believing it's all good, fun and helping us somehow.

Now, can you also consider the flip side of this? Do you find yourself scanning to see what others have posted, shared or portrayed themselves as, and then judge them for it somehow? When we feel left out, unacknowledged or angered by what we see, we have let it land on us. It becomes personal, and we may become triggered by the perceived hurt or feelings these posts instill in us. Is it possible, in that moment, to instead turn your focus onto yourself and ask why you are feeling this way? What part of you requires validation, and why do you feel the need to have to be seen or acknowledged by others? Where do these feelings originate? Are you perhaps actually judging yourself somehow instead of them? In truth, when we judge others, we are also judging ourselves somehow. There may be a hidden belief or inner wound you have, and it can feel easier, at times, to cast blame or judgment onto others, rather than to look inside. We unconsciously choose to leave the issue hidden, instead justifying to ourselves that we are right or OK by seeing the "wrong" in others.

We create our days. Things occur around us all the time, and we choose how to engage with them or not. Technology absolutely has its place and is a wonderful tool in so many ways, yet it is when we are able to consciously choose how we engage in it and become aware of how we are actually internalizing it, that we then gain freedom and a sense of power over ourselves, as we no longer need the validation. Therefore, it no longer defines us.

Here are a few things to ponder about your screen time. Please be honest with yourself and sit with each question for a moment. I found that my initial thoughts were not always my reality, but instead a belief I told myself. Becoming aware of yourself, your patterns and how they actually make you feel, brings with it the possibilities of change, and although change is not always easy or welcomed, it is imperative to grow.

- Does what you engage in bring joy into your day? Or does it simply add more mind clutter, worry or frustration?

- How much screen time do you engage in? Does it limit time for other things that you also deem important?

- Do you judge yourself or others when watching, listening or reading things online? And do you carry those feelings with you and allow them to affect yourself, your relationships or your day?

When you carry past events into your now, you are not able to be present or embrace where you are. You are instead reliving what happened earlier. This can affect how you show up during your day or how you engage with others moving forward, as you are unknowingly carrying the negative energy with you.

There are many things in our lives that we have no control over ... how we spend our time is not one of them.

We always have a choice. Time is a precious gift, both to share with the ones we love and to take in ourselves by embracing our day and the beauty that surrounds us. Sometimes we get caught up in the fun of social media, and that's OK. Yet, can you see the forest for the trees? Yes, it may be fun and is totally OK to engage in, but is it taking valuable time from someone or something that is really important in your life? Do you find you get involved in the drama of it all and take it with you in your day? Are you missing out on whole conversations while visiting with a friend or talking to your children because you are on social media at the same time?

ARE YOU PRESENT?

Finding ease in your day and deciding how you spend your time begins and ends with you. Gaining self-awareness and choosing to focus consciously on what you would like to create moving forward are both key. Implementing small steps or shifting your habits can and will create big change!

I'm going to be honest and say that I am not currently on social media. I will be one day, perhaps. I was simply not interested in it when I was married and then during and after my divorce I did not have the head space or desire to look at it. Instead, I chose to solely focus on me. Getting my mind from the hamster wheel to being calm, present and conscious was my first priority and something I felt would not have been attainable while being on social media. Now it's simply a personal choice to remain off, as I prefer the peace I've reached and have come to enjoy.

If you too would like more peace in your life, then become curious of where you are placing your focus. Are you consciously choosing?

RETHINKING LISTS

Life can feel incredibly busy with an array of things we need to do to stay organized and to feel healthy and well—eat well, sleep, exercise and rest to name a few. Your body lets you know what you need and when you need it, but do you listen? We can feel dog-tired and yet tell ourselves we have to or should do something or be somewhere. But do we really have to? Where do these thoughts originate? What would really happen if we didn't do them?

When I was growing up every Saturday was cleaning day, and the rule was you could not do anything else or go out until your part was finished. I didn't really think about it then because it wasn't hard and it was just part of the routine. However, now I am able to see the slight rigidity in it. There was never an alternate way suggested or allowed with regards to achieving a clean house. It was simply done this way and on this day. Looking back, I can see that on the upside, now as an adult, I have always been good at cleaning. On the downside, I sometimes found that I couldn't allow myself to have fun until things were done. We can at times carry old beliefs, patterns or habits with us into our now, and without awareness they may affect how we act, react or think we should be.

Lists are great to keep things on schedule and organized, and they can give you a sense of accomplishment when finished. They are definitely needed at times in life. Yet, if you feel frustrated or overwhelmed by them, you might want to look at how flexible you are. Do you feel controlled by lists? Do you feel guilty, stuck or anxious when they are altered or not completed? If so, do you know why? Are you able to feel a sense of accomplishment when something is crossed off your list, or do you find you are always behind the eight ball, unhappy with what you've done or where you are, thinking that you or what you have achieved is still not enough somehow? Where does this voice come from?

It's easy sometimes to get upset about things when we feel overwhelmed. It's in those moments that things can seem to be more urgent. Yes, there are certain things that need to be done in a certain time frame and in a certain way, but does everything? Is the urgency real or is it a story that your mind is telling you? Meaning, is it an old belief or pattern from your past that you now hold as truth? Are you in fact creating your own sense of chaos?

Consider these questions:

- What would *really* happen if you chose to shift, change or eliminate doing something?

- Can you allow yourself to stop long enough to find joy in your day and in what you are doing?

- Do you silently judge yourself somehow or do you believe others will? What are you afraid of?

When there is a sense of urgency, there is simply a fear attached. We unconsciously believe that our actions or inability to act will somehow affect us, or that they will affect how we will be perceived by others. When we do so, we are coming from a place of lack, and our minds have attached our worth somehow to our abilities or decision making. Alternatively, when we decide from a place of conscious awareness and presence, we are instead able to embrace what's in front of us with more lightheartedness and with a sense of calm. Although we still may need to do things—tasks don't just go away—this calm allows us to feel less worry around them. If you can, allow yourself to find stillness in your day, even if it's only for a few moments. Take a few deep breaths, then focus on something joyful. This helps clear mind clutter, releases stress and brings you back into the now, allowing you to see your day or options more clearly. It is always a good practice to pause and remind yourself: *Every day is a gift to experience and be grateful for.*

The Power of Intentional Creating

As you begin to grow in conscious awareness and see how you move through your days, you then have the opportunity to shift and create anew for yourself. What would you like to create, shift or change? And what is stopping you? Remember, the universe is limitless, which means you are too!

Aligning your energy with the energy of what you desire is key. If you desire more love, then being and feeling it within you, opening your heart to it and knowing you are worthy of it will attract more to you. Abundance and love can show up in various ways in our lives, and not only in the ways we think or believe they should. When we ask for more of either, it can show up in a smile from a stranger, a hug from a child or from witnessing an amazing sunset. These are all things that allow us to feel fulfilled and love in our hearts, thus abundant. If you desire more peace in your life, becoming aware of how the energy of it feels in your body and what aligns you with it is also key to attaining it. What steps can you take to feel more peace within yourself and your life? Simply begin to take notice of and bring awareness to how you feel inside during the day. For you can be sitting in a tranquil setting and still feel chaos fluttering within. Equally, when your energy is one of peace, you can find yourself in drama or chaos and yet remain peaceful and grounded.

Seeing yourself with what you desire now in the present, even if you don't have it yet, is telling the universe that you believe it is yours and you are worthy of having it. Taking action is what leads you there. Using the words, "I am," "I can" or "I will" to start positive statements can aid in creating a "can do" attitude within. Alternatively, using the words, "I can't," "I don't" or "I never" will create lower energy within you and therefore keep you in lack and possibly attract more of the same. So, whether you are wanting to become more present by unplugging, releasing stress, letting go of something, or if you are wanting to achieve or create something new in your life, see yourself doing it, having it or feeling it now. This creates your desired change or new reality.

As I began writing this, I remembered a time in my life long ago and how I had created what I wanted, although unknowingly at the time. We all have a level of conscious awareness and are continually evolving and growing as we move forward through our lives, gaining more as we go. Although I did not realize that I was creating at the time, looking back, everything worked out perfectly. I am now able to see that maybe I did have a strong inner knowing and perhaps more awareness than I realized.

I was a full-time mom until my kids both reached school age, and then I decided I would go back to work casually. I had strong stipulations in doing so though, and was often reminded by others that my thoughts were unrealistic.

I felt very strongly about what I wanted. Yes, I did desire to work outside the home, yet I did not wish to do so at the expense of my children. I wanted to find a job that allowed me to work while they were in school and yet be able to pick them up and be home with them the rest of the day, as well as on school holidays. To some, the thought of doing or asking for this was unheard of and unattainable. And I guess in some jobs it would be, yet I wanted it if I was to consider going back to work. I had worked full time at a bank prior to having children and had what I considered to be a good rapport with most people, so I made a few calls to touch base and let them know that I was ready to work and expressed when I was available. To me it seemed simple: it was their choice whether to hire me or not, just as it was mine to accept what they offered or not.

Long story short is that in returning to the bank, I was blessed to get exactly what I desired. Most days, I worked the hours my children were in school and finished in time to pick them up. I worked from September to the end of June and had Christmas break, spring break and the entire summer to be with my family. For this, I was incredibly thankful.

I have come to understand now that I created this for myself and my family. Being home for my kids was always at the forefront—it truly was the most important thing to me. We did not have an exuberant amount of money at the time to achieve this, yet I knew that somehow, it would all work out. And it did!

When you create from a place of love and trust that you are OK, you will be!

BE YOUR OWN KIND OF BEAUTIFUL

Affirmations can be very helpful in shifting and refocusing your mind from negative to positive. The words can have a powerful effect on you and your inner world, for as you focus you are bringing new awareness into your mind and body, and you are slowly shifting your old beliefs and patterns.

Like we covered earlier, a lot of affirmations begin with the words "I am," which when repeated, reaffirm to yourself that they are true and rebuild a new foundation for how you see yourself. However, truthfully, affirmations are not generally phrases that we say to ourselves often or easily. I'm not sure about you, but I have always found it easier to remind others how beautiful they are and how much I love them, compared to saying these things to myself.

When deciding to bring a new tool into your days, it's important to do so with kid gloves. With an understanding and acceptance of where you are in the moment and allow yourself to be as you are. Repetition is key, even if the words don't resonate with you in the beginning; for each time you repeat them, you are shifting and reprogramming your mind. In time, you will begin to feel the energy of each word as truth.

Personally, I began implementing affirmations slowly. At first, I just listened to them because I found the words didn't want to flow out of my mouth easily, or sometimes at all. As time passed I started to see progress. The words began to flow with a bit more ease, although I found I still wasn't quite believing them. So I decided to move to the next step, which was saying them in front of the mirror while looking at myself. I found that there is definitely a stronger connection to yourself as you say the words this way. One of the first times that I looked into my own eyes and repeated the affirmations, I was surprised when I felt emotional and began welling up. Tears rolled down my face as I told myself, "I love you," "You are worthy," and "I am proud of you." These were words that I deemed to be untrue at the time, and they triggered the subconscious parts of me that needed healing—thus the tears.

My reaction allowed me to see that I wanted and needed more positive ways and things around me to help me refocus and shift. So I wrote down my affirmations and other positive phrases on sticky notes and placed them on my fridge and bedroom mirror. The way I looked at it was, the more I surrounded myself with positive things, the more opportunities I would have to see them and refocus.

Here are a few of the affirmations that became part of my days. I added to and changed them around regularly, depending on how I was feeling and what I felt I needed.

- Just B r e a t h e.

- I like who I see in the mirror.

- I am loving, loved and lovable.

- I have amazing inner strength.

- You Matter.

- Be gentle with yourself. You are ALWAYS doing the best that you can.

- You Are Enough.

- I am content and at ease.

- I AM OK.

- I am beautiful inside and out.

Affirmations can also be used in sets. This set of three is an intimate way of bringing confidence into your days:

- Yes, I can…

- Yes, I will…

- Yes, I am…

Simply fill in the end word or words with whatever you are needing to hear or believe in the moment or would like to manifest moving forward. Every time you repeat any of these statements, either out loud or in your mind, you are creating new positive thoughts and reaffirming how strong, capable and worthy you are, thereby shifting and releasing old beliefs. Remember:

You choose what kind of day you will have and how you will show up in it.

Chapter 4

What Was I Thinking?

CONNECTING THE DOTS

"We are responsible for and create our own reality," were the first words I heard coming from the instructor in a mindful meditation class I was in a few years ago. I was still fairly fresh into being separated then, and I vividly remember thinking, *What?* as I turned and looked her way before my body suddenly froze. My mind seemed to shut down for a moment, and therefore did not hear her words that immediately followed. My many thoughts instead began swirling around inside my mind, defending what I had perceived her as saying: that I was to blame and that I somehow could have changed my situation. It took every ounce of strength in me to not shout out, "Are you kidding me?" There was no way—in my mind—that I had created or wanted this to be happening in my life. Thankfully I didn't, because I was able to calm my insides down and listen to the rest of her teachings. She continued to say that although we have no control over other people's actions or over situations that occur because of other people, we *do* have control over ourselves, over how and what we think, over how we react and over how we let their actions land on us. More importantly, we have the choice and ability to either hang onto the anger, grief, resentment or whatever kind of upset we feel because of a perceived wrong, OR we can realize that when we do that, the only person we are hurting is ourselves, and we can instead allow all that negative energy to move through us and release it.

This lesson would begin a slow shift in me, as I began allowing my focus (consciousness) to move from past events and place it onto myself. How was I experiencing it all? And why? I would find it was not an immediate or easy shift and one that would need time and patience to navigate through.

We apparently have approximately sixty thousand thoughts per day. Most of them don't land on us. There's maybe only a thousand per day that we are actually aware of, but that's still a lot. Every thought that we believe is true, we will then experience. But what is a belief, *really*? A belief is simply a story we tell ourselves over and over again until we believe it's true. It is only your thoughts, and although it can feel very true to you, it doesn't mean it is. It is not an eternal truth. We all create in two ways. We either believe it, see it and create it OR we are unconscious and on autopilot, and we will still create and experience things, which can sometimes be the moments when we wonder, *How did that happen?* Or think, *Hmm, I didn't see that coming.* The good thing is we can always choose again.

During the day there can be many instances when we feel tense, upset or react negatively to a situation or person, but we just continue moving through our day. We don't stop to notice what's actually happening within us in those moments. Yet, if we could stop, we would be able to see exactly what is happening quickly within us. You have a thought—which gives you an emotion—then you tell yourself a story around it—this fills your body with more of that emotion and sensations that helps you to justify or defend how you are feeling, thus believing the story you are telling yourself. This all occurs within seconds. The longer you stay in the story, the more you can get emotionally charged and begin to go down what I call the rabbit hole. This can easily happen as the story becomes more and more exaggerated in your mind, and your emotions continue to rise and intensify. Your thoughts become overwhelming and continual, and it feels like you are in a hole that you can't get out of or stop digging.

An example of this could be if I told you I don't like your new haircut. That statement could have you thinking something along the lines of: *What? Really? How rude! Why not?* These thoughts then connect with your self-esteem and self-worth, which fills you with doubt, triggering thoughts like: *Oh wow, I do look ugly. Why did I change my haircut? I knew I should've left it alone.* The story you tell yourself fills your body with the emotions and sensations that only intensify your already negative feelings. Your body may suddenly contract, your stomach or throat can tighten up and this concoction of emotion validates the story you are telling yourself. Depending on how strongly you are triggered, you could then react harshly and project this emotion onto me, somehow blaming me for saying that I didn't like your hair, which then has the potential to affect our friendship. If you stay in the story and emotion long enough, you might find you feel more justified for your actions. In time, this can become your conclusion—your story that you now believe is true of why our friendship changed. For most of us, this all happens unconsciously. We are unable to see that it all started with a single thought that triggered something inside of us. An old hurt or belief about ourselves from our past that we unconsciously buried, rises up in us as a result, and we then react accordingly. This is how we create our own reality.

If you can, stop and consider what might happen if you were able to instead catch the trigger before it grabs hold of you; to become aware or conscious of it as it's happening and instead feel or sense the discord in your body and allow it to move through you without the urge to react. How could that potentially change or shift your experience?

It's always easier for us to find blame in others, and we all do it. But the truth is, it's not about anyone else or whether they have acted appropriately or not. Everyone is responsible for themselves. The key instead is to turn inwards and look at yourself and why or what triggered you. That's when the true healing begins. Be aware of your bodily sensations when you find yourself triggered, notice how you feel as a result and ask yourself, "What am I thinking?" This begins to connect the mind and body and illuminates how we indeed do create our days. If you could then stop, breathe and say, OK, yes, they did do this, or this did happen, but why does it bother me? How am I letting it land on me? What am I feeling? Thinking? And are my thoughts the truth or a story I'm telling myself? This switches your focus from blaming others and feeling like a victim, and brings it back to you. It begins to change the narrative in your mind, which allows you to feel more in control of yourself.

Remember, you cannot change others' opinions, thoughts, beliefs or actions. You can however, look at them as signs to guide you towards becoming more aware, conscious and connected to yourself. Each time you notice your bodily sensations and connect with your thoughts, you not only gain awareness, but you also lessen the negative energy associated with the trigger a little more. You are then able to uncover the truth—the real and perhaps hidden story of why you feel upset.

Feeling like a victim is just that—a feeling. It is created in our minds and is our own story we tell ourselves about how something played out. And the more we ruminate on it, the more we believe it. We can then use it to justify our actions and defensiveness we display. Over time the victim mentality can become who we think we are, a part of our personalities and how we view ourselves.

During my divorce, whether I found myself down the rabbit hole, in the heat of the moment or in a puddle of tears, it was quite challenging to notice anything internally. I somehow felt validated to feel this way, and as a result would find myself casting blame everywhere else, which left me in a state of despair. I felt stuck. Nothing made sense to me, and the stories I told myself were continually negative and self-sabotaging. I can now see that this kept me in low energy and very much feeling like a victim. I was unable to see that I was hurting myself by keeping past events alive. It was simply where and who I was at the time. This healing, as with all others, was a process and I am now aware that in order to begin to see the light, you sometimes first have to be in darkness.

Although I could not change others' actions, the past or my present situations, my awareness was showing me that I could change how I experience them, thus growing trust in my own inner power.

This is a process, and one that requires patience, understanding, practice and, above all, love for yourself. Seeing, feeling or noticing that you were triggered after you've reacted or while in the midst of reacting are sometimes the first steps. With practice and growing awareness, you will begin to notice and catch it before you react. In the meantime, celebrate the fact that you did notice, and any other small successes along the way.

Yesterday I was clever,
so I wanted to change the world.
Today I am wise, so I am CHANGING MYSELF.

—RUMI

The Stuff That Gets in Our Way

I was beginning to see my limited beliefs, wounds and patterns. The stories I once believed were true shifted a little each day. I placed my consciousness on positive things and retold myself the truth of my story, which in turn began to alter the conclusion. The new conclusion would become my new belief in time.

I felt the effects of my new beliefs when it came to the following aspects of my life:

1. **SELF-SABOTAGE.** We speak to ourselves on a daily basis without even realizing it. We might be telling ourselves: "I'm so stupid; I'll never learn that," or "I'm so fat/skinny; I hate my body," or "What do I have to offer? They wouldn't want me!" We might also have thoughts like: *I'm not worthy of love, I'll never measure up,* or *I wish I could be more like them.* These are only a sample of the many ways we may talk and think about ourselves. What we don't realize is that when the words are repeated out loud or in our minds, over time they become how we actually think and believe we are. Words are energy, and what we speak or think will become our experience and how we will feel. It's the law of attraction: we attract back to us the same energy we put out. So, if we keep telling ourselves how stupid we are, we will not only feel stupid, but we may not want to apply ourselves for lack of self-esteem or confidence. Over time, this has the potential to attract situations and people to you that will enforce this belief.

   Become aware of how you speak about yourself, whether it's to another or to yourself. Say the word "cancel" each time you catch yourself saying or thinking something negative to or about yourself.

I did this and WOW, I was amazed at how many times I was having to say "cancel." Who knew?

It's important to note that whether we are sabotaging ourselves or sabotaging our life possibilities with our words, we have the power to change them. As I gained new awareness of how I spoke negatively to myself, I also started to recognize how I spoke my desires out loud. I noticed that more often than not I would say what I didn't want in my life, instead of actually stating what it is I did want. The truth is it's all so automatic that we simply have no idea we are doing it until we bring our awareness to it. So, when I caught myself stating what I *don't* want in my life or for myself, I would choose to rephrase my words to state what I *do* want in a more positive way.

The truth is, anything negative we speak about ourselves or to ourselves is one hundred percent not true. Why? Remember, we are made up of expansion, light and harmony at our truest form—we are all beautiful, glorious spiritual human beings!

2. **BAD STARTS.** How our day starts usually lays the groundwork for the rest of it, right? If you sleep in, you may be in an instant panic, thinking about how this messes up your whole day's plans. You don't have time for breakfast, you run out the door forgetting your lunch on the counter, you take a supposedly

faster route to work only to be met with construction roadblocks; your body is filled with anxiety before you even get to work. This lower energy you embody then attracts more of the same to you, creating your perceived "bad" day.

If you could stop and simply take a moment to just breathe slowly and become present, it can break the negative cycle you find yourself in. It doesn't change the stressful situation, but it changes you, because you shift your energy in that moment. Once you've done so, you may then find you are able to move forward more calmly and meet the day with more ease.

During my divorce, I remember driving to work when I was not feeling very happy at all. I didn't know how I would ever get through the day. I would tell myself as I drove, "I am happy," or "My day will be fun and full of laughter," or maybe simply, "I'm OK." Whatever I felt I needed was what I'd go with. I would repeat it several times on my way, and what I found is that it raised my energy from lower to higher, even just a little, and some of the "not so good" stuff that did happen during the day didn't really land on me as negatively as it otherwise might have. Throughout my day I would also implement positive reminders to myself, "I am worthy", "Everything is OK," "I am enough."

3. **RUMINATION.** The continual cycle of thoughts and stories that keeps your mind on fast-forward and unable to stop is called rumination. It's your mind trying to make sense of and find the logic in an illogical situation. When this becomes continual, it can easily become a pattern we adapt to. It will keep the story you tell yourself alive with all the possible scenarios that could happen, should happen or did happen and all the what ifs, maybes and doubts that only add fuel to the fire encompassing your mind. This process will undoubtedly only keep fear alive within you. It will in all likelihood lead to reacting versus responding (unconsciously instead of consciously) when you are triggered, or it may leave you feeling stuck and unable to make what would otherwise be easy decisions. Ruminating feels like you are on a hamster wheel in your mind that just keeps going round and round.

The truth may be that you don't know the whole story or the real truth of the situation, but your mind is trying to make sense of it all anyways to protect, justify or maybe defend you somehow. The ego is a vital part of us and can keep us feeling structured and safe at times, but the truth is, it also lives in lack and fear. This fear is how anxiousness, upset or defensiveness arise within us. When we are in our ego mind, what we have, want or long for is never quite enough, which leaves us usually striving for more. This can then translate back to us that we too are not enough. The ego resides in our Solar Plexus Chakra, or the mental chakra as I call it, and it makes sense that when this Chakra is open and flowing, our thoughts are healthier and more balanced and loving without our ego attached. We feel clearer in our minds, and decision making may feel easier to do. Guided meditations, finding stillness within your day and breathing techniques absolutely help this process.

4. **OUR LIMITED BELIEFS AND PATTERNS.** We've adopted many beliefs and patterns of behaviour throughout our lives, whether they come from our childhoods, teachers, peers, ancestral family roles, family origins or media. We also all hold many roles in our lives, including ones like mom, dad, wife, husband, daughter, son, employee or employer. These roles contribute to our beliefs and patterns as well, as we may have been taught that the people in each of these roles should act in a certain way. All of these things and the people we engage with during our days are telling us directly or indirectly what we "should" be, do or have in our lives. If we believe these things to be true, they can slowly diminish our own thoughts and lower our self-esteem. In time, this may leave us feeling like we are not enough as we are. There is an abundance of information in the world that comes

from different sources, and we do have a choice of what we focus on and how we let it land on or affect us.

Presence and consciousness awareness are key, for they keep you in the now and separate you from any chaos that is either in or around you. The truth is *no one can make* you feel anything unless you give them permission to. We put our own walls up, and we can take them down. Have you ever wondered why you believe this or that? Why do you follow the words of another and hold them as truth? Ask yourself, "Is what I'm thinking real? Is it what I *really* believe? Where did it come from, and is it true?" Take note of how it feels in your body when you consider these things.

Unknowingly, we often listen, take in and believe that which others say is true, when in reality, they may be projecting their own limited beliefs or patterns onto us. And when we believe their beliefs, it can limit how we choose to move forward, see ourselves or view the world.

A couple of years ago, I read a story, which is a good example of how we create our lives. It clearly depicts how our thoughts, patterns and beliefs create our lives, and how our control of these things can help us rewrite our own conclusions. The key elements of the story are about twin boys who grew up with an alcoholic and abusive father. The father was unfortunately unable to show love to either of the boys during their childhoods and eventually landed himself in jail because of the abuse. When the boys reached adulthood, they had become two totally different people leading totally different lives. Their mother was curious why they were so different, so she reached out to talk to each one. The first son had lived most of his teenage years in trouble with alcohol and drugs, like his father, which continued into his adulthood and, yes, eventually landed himself in jail too. When his mom asked him why he was the way he was, his response was, "I had no choice, look at Dad." The second son was happy and felt good about himself and his life. He was married with children of his own and had secured a good job and a nice home. When his mom asked him how he had achieved this in his life he said, "I had no choice. I'm not Dad."

The first son undoubtedly felt unloved and like a victim throughout his childhood, a mentality that ultimately led him to feel helpless to change, thereby leading him to the same life as his father. His story became his why and justified who he became. The second son saw his dad for who he was and, more importantly, regained his own worth. He was able to see that he was not his father, he was able to heal from the hurt he incurred in the past and he consciously chose to reclaim his adult life, knowing he deserved better. He changed his story.

What we experience throughout our lives is at times out of our control, and it moulds our minds, bodies and spirits as we grow into adults. Unconsciously, we push down and choose not to work through certain things because we deem them too hurtful, painful, scary or wrong in some way. We bury them in our subconscious because we don't want to think about them or look at them. We think they are gone because out of sight, out of mind, right? Not necessarily. Like the story above reveals, these things are still in us, and the energy of them can become stuck. We then carry these beliefs, patterns and energies with us into our futures. The universe will always remind us of our unhealed parts in various ways, such as through the people and experiences we encounter. However, it's our choice when or if we are willing to see these parts, to really look at them and heal them.

It's important to note that there can also be things that only happen once in your life, yet may deeply affect you; it's not always a lifetime of accumulated events that drag us down. Either way, if you allow that hurt to fester, and it becomes your story, you too may find that you feel like a victim. The truth is, these traumas we endure briefly or continually are not who we are, and they cannot define us or become us unless we allow them to remain in us, unhealed.

The fears we don't face become our limits

—ROBIN SHARMA

Subconscious Pain and Triggers

Everyone has them! Think of your subconscious like a computer, and all the files added are your patterns and beliefs deep inside you from all of your life experiences until now. These files consist of all of the hurtful things you've felt or experienced in life that you pushed down, disregarded or chose to not look at. These are things that you think are gone because you might have told yourself, "I don't care anymore," or, "It doesn't matter; I'm OK." Yet, when a similar situation occurs or someone says or does something that reminds you of the hurt associated with that pain, you become triggered. You can have a very strong emotion, very quickly. Even if the actual situation appears different on the outside, the emotions around it are felt in very much the same way. Sometimes you may not know why something or someone bothers you, yet they do.

The subconscious wounds we carry are usually associated with feelings of our own worth or self-esteem. Perhaps we are not pretty, smart or capable enough; there is a long list of possible "not enoughs". We may be triggered when we feel disrespected, judged, left out, unloved or hurt and not really understand why, leading us to blame or project this pain onto others. Have you ever stopped and asked yourself, "Why do I feel this way? Why do the words or actions of others bother me or land on me?" The feelings that grab us when we are triggered, although unpleasant or perhaps even painful, give us a chance to look at why they are there and what is really underneath them. Become curious and ask yourself, "When have I felt this way before?" It may take a bit of time to understand what is really beneath your reaction. Is it from your past? And if so, how and why is it affecting you today? Who do you become when you are triggered? Or is there perhaps a part of you that you are choosing to leave hidden?

When triggered, it's important to notice how you feel. Allow the energy (bodily sensations that arise) to move through you and out of you, then remind yourself of the truth around your thoughts or experience. Remember, it's OK to feel however you are feeling in any given situation. Simply acknowledge and validate each feeling and allow them to be as they are. Notice your thoughts. Are they true? Or a story you believe? Then reaffirm to yourself what you are needing to hear, whether that is "I am safe," "I am OK," "I am beautiful/smart/capable," or simply, "I am enough." When repeated, this dissipates the negative energy and lessens its hold on you a little more each time.

When left unhealed, the wounds we embody and their associated energies stay with us as we move through our days. Therefore, they will undoubtedly show up again and again in the hopes that you will shine a light on them and heal them.

What is Shadow Work
Shadow work is the process of
exploring your inner darkness
or "shadow self".
Shadow work uncovers every part of yourself
that has been disowned, repressed and rejected.
It is one of the most authentic paths to enlightenment.

—LONERWOLF

The following is an event in my life that I had buried and unknowingly took with me as I grew up into adulthood.

One summer evening many years ago, when I was a little girl, I was in a car with my parents and two sisters. We were driving on a country dirt road when my dad decided to turn off his headlights and speed down the road in total darkness. I think he thought it was funny. There were no street lights to show us the road, and I kept on trying to widen my eyes as big as they could go, wishing I would somehow be able to see. But try as I might, I could not see the road at all. It was so black that my hand was not visible in front of me. I curled up in a ball in the back seat, quietly sobbing, feeling alone as my body trembled with fear. It was only dark for a few moments before my dad turned the headlights back on, but it felt like a lifetime to me. There was never a word spoken about it or concern of how I felt afterwards. It was like it hadn't happened.

As life continued and I grew up, I found I would feel a sense of uneasiness or anxiety if I had to go somewhere and didn't know the way there. If I couldn't see it in my mind, I would feel an instant pit in my stomach. I would find myself asking others what their plans were, as I somehow needed reassurance of my own capabilities to get there and that I would be OK. It was annoying to me, and I did not understand why I felt this way. As I became an adult, the anxiety grew and I found I felt immediately triggered by the thought of going somewhere without clear directions, and it would show up in me as straight-up fear. I would actually feel sick to my stomach and at times find myself in an instant panic when faced with situations like these. This fear was unconsciously projected outwards to others as they tried to reassure me, or worse laughed, because they couldn't understand why I was reacting this way. Sounds crazy I know because I was an adult, yet it was very real to me. I couldn't explain it to anyone because I didn't know why myself. In fact, I had no idea why until a few years ago when I began working on my own shadows (subconscious things I had buried) and the memory of the drive was brought back into my awareness.

I had been meditating daily for quite some time, becoming more in tune with my mind and body, and had become aware of the fear within me that was showing up in various ways and at different times. So I asked the universe where this fear was coming from. Then one day, seemingly out of nowhere, I was answered. I was standing in front of my mirror, getting ready to go out when it came to me. It felt like a sudden flash of memory being downloaded into my mind and body—the memory of being that little girl in the back seat of the car. Within moments, I found myself on the floor, my body curled in the fetal position in a puddle of my own tears, feeling like I was once again in the back seat of the car. The feelings were so intense as I lay on the floor. I could feel the fear that I had felt that day invade my body with every tear that fell. When my tears eased up, I stood up and looked at myself in the mirror. My eyes were puffy and black as my mascara had run down my face and I felt an immense feeling of true compassion for the person I saw in the mirror: ME! I wrapped my arms around myself and gave the little girl inside of me a hug that had been much-needed a long time ago and never felt. I told myself, "It's OK. I've got you." "Yes, that was a very scary day; it was not your fault." I then reminded myself of my truth now: "It's OK to release this fear, I am safe!"

As I sat with this revelation, I was able to see the connection between the experience and the fear I had brought with me as I grew up, and ultimately how it manifested into my now. I was in darkness that day many years ago and could not see in front of me or the road ahead, feeling frightened, alone and unloved. These same feelings would resurface each and every time I felt unclear of my way, leaving me as an adult now, feeling inadequate and fearful. I was unaware that these feelings were actually opportunities for me to look at myself and why the fear was there.

This new awareness did not change, stop or make my fear disappear instantly. It did however, allow me to see the truth of it, so when it did show up in the future I was able to understand why it was there and I would be able to allow it to move through me more easily. By letting the energy move through me and reminding myself of the truth around it, the intense energy that I had previously experienced slowly decreased in time. This gave me a sense of having more control over myself and not being a victim to the fear. This is a practice I continue today. Although it rarely arises now, if I feel the fear show up, it's more of a discomfort. I am very aware that it's there, but I simply notice it, feel it and re-frame the story to tell myself one of reassurance and confidence. I then tell myself: "I love you." Deep wounds can take some time to clear, so try not to be discouraged as you become aware of yours. Remember that they are there to show you that they still need your awareness and love.

In a sense, this experience opened Pandora's box for me as I realized this event was definitely buried within me, as I had no recollection of it until that day. It also strengthened my connection to the universe as I knew I was indeed heard when I asked to be shown why my fear was there. So, I continued my quest to now look at each and every fearful or negative thought I had and the situations I found myself in with different eyes. I saw them as opportunities to become aware, not only of them but where they originated, how I internalized them and how I felt now as a result, so I could in time release them too. While working through this I experienced painful emotions and feelings that would arise in me. These feelings, at times could grab me or leave me feeling frozen, afraid, fearful or stuck for a bit, depending on the reason. But I would continually remind myself that I really am OK and that in order to truly heal them, I had to become aware of what needed healing. I'll be honest and say that this is something that I continue to work on today. Although I've acknowledged and released most of what no longer serves me (past beliefs, patterns and fear), there are still things that can arise. We are all continually growing and evolving, and therefore, there will always be things that still need my attention.

This process is something you will move through as you are ready. Feeling, acknowledging and releasing the associated energies and emotions that have attached to or now define you are steps in that process. Speak truth to your experiences and remind yourself that these parts of you are not who you truly are, but rather your inner wounds that need love, attention and healing.

Life is a beautiful journey with no real end, and the quest for love, presence and consciousness is a goal we all have, whether we are aware of it or not. As you too begin to look at yourself more deeply, have patience, have understanding and be willing to see yourself through the eyes of compassion. It can take extreme courage at times to acknowledge and face what we perhaps deemed as a weakness in ourselves, and it can at times leave us feeling quite vulnerable, guilty or shameful.

In those times, it's important to remember that:

They are only weaknesses if we choose to "think" of them that way.

There are many meditations, books and videos that can help as you move through this process. Releasing the negative emotions and energy, letting go of what no longer serves you and gaining self-love are all steps that may take time. Remember to always be gentle with yourself along the way.

The following are a few people that I resonated with and who were instrumental in guiding me as I moved through these stages of my journey:

- Louise Hay

- Eckhart Tolle

- Abraham Hicks

- Deepak Chopra

- Gabrielle Bernstein

- Fearless Soul

Two of my favourite books from Eckhart Tolle are: *A New Earth* and *The Power of Now*. To me, both are equally amazing! I have read and reread them both several times through the years, as each time I seem to gain more and higher wisdom from his teachings.

Chapter 5

Clearing The View

CREATING FROM OUR PAST

PERCEPTIONS are our own views of ourselves, our lives, situations or other people. They're in the eye of the beholder. They're viewed through the lens of the world in which we were born into—the time period and the people we are surrounded by; even the internet can affect how we see and think about things.

It's the reason why two people can watch the same movie at the same time and walk away feeling two different ways afterwards, having different opinions or views about it. Who is right? No one! There is no right or wrong. They are both seeing through their own eyes, and therefore may see it very differently. One person may be brought to tears while the other perhaps feels nothing at all.

Expectations are what we think should or will happen. We believe if I do this, then this will happen. By telling ourselves a story of what we expect, we have possibly set ourselves up for disappointment and potential heartache without realizing it. We are putting our hopes on something, someone, a situation or even ourselves without having any way of knowing the future outcome because the future is unknown.

Our perceptions and expectations of ourselves are who we believe we are, as well as who we believe we should be, what we should do and what we should have in our lives. At times we may feel like we're outside of ourselves looking in, wanting a part of ourselves or a part of our lives to be different somehow. We may be unconsciously trying to control how something will play out or how we show up with others, believing this will bring a certain desired outcome. This same unconscious nature can occur when we are focused on ourselves. There may be an actual part of your physical body that you wish was different, or maybe you feel envious of someone and wish you were more like them. All of these negative thoughts derive from our hidden lack that we feel within—our beliefs that we are somehow less because of someone, something or the way we appear.

Have you ever noticed how you feel when seeing someone else's good fortune? Are you able to feel happiness for them, or do you silently judge or resent them? Or yourself somehow? Have you ever stopped to wonder why you feel this way? What is it that you see or perceive in them or their lives that you believe is better than you or your life? That is the million-dollar question, for those feelings are the keys to look at. In order to feel true happiness for others and not judge or compare yourself to them, you first have to do and feel happiness within and for yourself. We need to access the "enough" part of ourselves. As you discover, accept and love who you are in all of your glory, your vibration will rise, and you will begin to see the truth: that they are not in fact better or have anything better than you, they are just having different experiences. You are always enough just as you are! Other people are only better in our minds if we believe and tell ourselves they are. So love yourself for who you are and not who you believe you should be.

Remember, we are all unique and that's a beautiful thing. If we were all the same how boring would that be? Learn to accept the part of you or your life that you deem to be "not enough" and send love to it. Become thankful for it. For it is not really the shape of your body or the perceived lack in your life that is behind your upset, but the ideas, thoughts and limited beliefs you tell yourself about them. If you look at a part of yourself with unhappy, unaccepting eyes, then you are resisting who and where you are and unconsciously telling yourself that you are not enough. This leaves you in lack, always wishing you could be different in some way. Granted, maybe a change in diet or exercise could be beneficial, as becoming healthier might aid in how you perceive yourself. However, it is also your internal dialogue and thoughts that are really longing for your loving attention.

Our beliefs and patterns from past experiences and how we perceive them or expect things to play out are intertwined and directly or indirectly play a role in how we see, believe and expect things or ourselves to be now. When we find ourselves stuck, we are simply not present. Instead, we are being led by the past, or we are worried about the future and unable to see what's in front of us. When we are coming from a state of lack or fear, we may unknowingly be setting limitations or restrictions for ourselves.

I saw a great example of how we create our now from past experiences portrayed in the TV show *Parenthood*, in the episode "I'm Cooler Than You Think". A young man named Crosby learns that he has a five-year-old son with a former girlfriend. Crosby is known for his fun-loving ways and for not always making the right decisions in his life, yet he embraces the boy and his former girlfriend and wants to create a sense of family with them. As they become closer, the former girlfriend has to leave town for a few weeks and decides to leave her son with her mother, who is not happy with the situation her daughter is in, or with her daughter's new man. It was this next part that I thought got to the heart of how we carry our thoughts and perceptions with us and how it affects our now and potentially our future. Crosby catches on and tells his son's grandmother that he feels like he is auditioning for her. She replies that her ex-husband was fun loving just like him and had left her after five years of marriage, and that she wasn't going to allow that to happen to her daughter. Crosby responds that she will have to accept him for who he is, because unlike her husband, he will not be going anywhere. He then goes on to tell her that although their thoughts and ideas around his son may look very different on the outside, their desired end goals are very much the same. The next scene shows the grandmother with Crosby and his son, all having fun together.

When we experience something hurtful, for example something caused by a particular person, and carry the pain with us, it can be easy to perceive others with the same qualities or traits in the same way. We build a protective wall around ourselves, not realizing that if it never comes down, we may be isolating ourselves.

Through the Years

Society has evolved throughout generations. How we see, do and expect things to be has also shifted or changed. How our parents grew up and what was expected of them is very different from how we grew up, and even more different from how our children grew up, and so forth. Every person has a view of how they lived and experienced their childhood and life, and for the most part, it's all they can see. I know I've often heard stories that start with, "In my day…"

When I was young, I can recall learning the importance of saving your money and that working hard was the best way to achieve the things you wanted in life. There were at times very rigid ways of looking at things collectively, as it was an era in which most people were led to only see the wrong way or the right way of how to do things. Very seldom would a middle ground or alternative view be discussed. The man was generally considered the "man of the house" and was for the most part, the breadwinner. Kids were expected to be seen, and for the most part not heard and expected to do what they were told, as it may be considered rude or talking back if they didn't. In school, teachers had free reign to use a yardstick or leather strap on you to keep you and the classroom in order. It is these past experiences that we carry with us as we grow up that create our own perceptions and experiences today.

We all learn from the generations before us. Family patterns and beliefs can be passed down and seen through each generation. Among these patterns and beliefs are lessons in wisdom, the meaning of family and how to love and be loved. We then internalize these teachings and form our own perceptions through our own eyes. I have come to understand that we are all doing the very best we can, given our level of consciousness, our life experiences and the wounds we carry within. Everyone can only give from where they are, what they know and believe.

Our grandparents or parents may have experienced war, racism or poverty when they were younger. They may have lived through times in history when there were very rigid ideas and beliefs developed by fear, perhaps as a form of survival. Trauma, who they were as a person, or not having enough food or shelter growing up can instill a sense of fear and lack within, and they unknowingly carry the fear with them moving forward into adulthood. It is through these eyes that the next generation, (us) are then taught, and therefore the cycle continues. As parents, we have no idea that we too embody this negative energy and that we are transferring it to our children, as we think we are protecting them and showing them love. Our decisions come from our heart, we think, as we are totally unaware of what is really guiding them. For example, as parents, we seem to always want more for our children. We want them to have what we lacked or needed more of as children, whether that be love, attention, possessions or a happy home. We want them to be safe! And that's a beautiful thing—when it's given with a pure heart. However, more often than not, we are being driven unconsciously, unaware that we are following family patterns that may have been built around fear and trauma. Yet, this could change, if we chose more consciously. Seeing our parents or grandparents with awareness, love and understanding allows us to shift our thoughts and see that they too are just like us. People trying to do the best they can with what they know at the time. And, if our choices were instead made through conscious awareness, not fear, we would be able to clearly see the old patterns and beliefs as they arise in us and choose to heal and release them. Then we would be able to clearly see, feel and decide what our truth is and move forward more conscious and aware.

How do you know what energies (negative or positive) you are *really* carrying? Simply become aware of how you feel as you speak. Do you feel content and at ease, or do you feel out of sorts somehow? What is driving your words, decisions or thoughts? Is it your heart or your limited beliefs? Is there a fear attached? Remember that it's OK if you find yourself in the ego, because that awareness gives you the opportunity to heal and release it. You then have the option to look inside and find a way to give yourself what you are needing.

The more I illuminated the patterns and limited beliefs that I had carried into the present and understood where they originated, the easier it became to shift and release the energy of them. This in turn allowed me to give myself the love and forgiveness that I needed. It also opened the door for understanding and compassion for others as well. Again, everyone can only give from where they are and their own level of awareness and consciousness. We cannot change our past, the choices we made, or the ones of others. We can now however, choose again!

The following are a couple of common beliefs or patterns you may notice or feel you carry:

- Having a strong work ethic is good, right? Yes, it is. Being passionate about what you do can feel amazing. Yet, it's important to also look at what is behind your drive. How do your thoughts around your work ethic make you feel? Do you find you're setting unreachable goals for yourself? Or do you define yourself by your achievements, or lack of them? In other words, are you being driven by the ego or your soul's desire? Living in the ego will not allow you to truly be happy where you are, and it will keep you believing you need more or have to be more. This self-judgment can then be projected towards others as you may begin to judge them for their lifestyle choices and decisions. Alternatively, living from your soul's desire may not seem to give you the immediate results you want, yet each step will feel right and like you are where you are meant to be. The truth is, we are always where we are meant to be in any moment, even when it doesn't feel like it. And we all have our own lessons to learn and our own path to travel. What we take and learn or how we grow from each experience is what brings us closer to understanding this truth. So become curious. What feels good to you? Where is your soul calling you to go? Are you listening?

- Saving money is a great thing to do, right? Yes, it is. Although, how much is enough? If fear of spending or thoughts of never having enough money creep in or stop you from enjoying the fruits of your labour, they may limit you and how you live. Also, it's important to remember that money is energy, and so whatever energy we associate with money—negative, positive, low or high—we will attract more of the same into our lives. When we live in a lack mindset, we will potentially experience more of that. Equally, when we are grateful for what we do have, it invites more to flow to us. When we feel abundant, we simply are abundant.

- Doing everything the "proper" way is good, right? Yes, it is. Yet, when you believe there is only one right way or wrong way of doing things, or tell yourself you're a perfectionist, you really only hurt yourself. For it is when we unconsciously carry and believe limited beliefs and patterns about how we "should be seen" or be that we can have a rigid way of thinking. It can feel like you are stuck in a box with no room to open up the top for expansion or growth. You become unable to or unwilling to change for fear of doing something wrong or worry of how you will be seen or perceived by others. Fear of always being seen as perfect puts undue pressure on you. You may be unaware of this fear within you, as you may also believe this is "just the way you are". Maybe you have always set the bar high for your own expectations of yourself. You may feel you have to do something a particular way or be a certain way. If you notice that you feel this way, it's ok, awareness is the first step. Understanding where these rigid beliefs came from, is the next.

I invite you to ask yourself why you feel you have to be seen as perfect or right. What is *really* at the bottom of this fear? Where does it stem from? Is it your belief or is it an expectation that was passed down through your family? If it is a family pattern, ask yourself, *Is it really what I believe or want for myself? Am I really happy being this way?* And, if not, can you now begin to shift it? Meaning, can you be willing to see that you are enough, just as you are, without the validation from others? If not, why is that? What are you gaining by being perceived as perfect or right? Can you instead begin to give yourself what you are needing?

Unknowingly, family patterns and beliefs can be continually carried through generations when we are unconscious and unaware that they are in us. It is only when we allow ourselves to stop and take the time to bring awareness and understanding to them and begin to see ourselves through the lens of love that things begin to shift or change. Remember fear, unless warranted, is a feeling that our mind can create, so we can choose to see it and take steps to release it.

Seeing Ourselves Clearly

When we stay stuck, concerned about others or judge either ourselves or them for their actions, we are then in lack within ourselves and we feel powerless. This lower energy feeling then creates how we experience our present and our days moving forward.

So, why do you *really* choose to do or not do something? For myself, I've found that expectations from others, doing something because everyone else was or wanting to be perceived as good or nice have all driven me in the past. I used to feel very guilty if I chose differently than others because I felt I wasn't doing what I "should" be doing, or I felt afraid that I would be judged for my decisions. At first, seeing these aspects of myself and why I felt this way were not easy things to look at. Although, as I gained self-awareness I began to realize that they were not a "bad" part of me, nor was I "bad" for having them. They were simply beliefs, patterns and aspects of myself that needed some love and attention, and after my initial thoughts of self-judgment, that's how I decided to think of them moving forward.

Being willing to look at the good, the bad and the ugly parts of yourself with compassionate eyes allows you to then begin healing and releasing the parts of you that no longer serve you. You can begin to shine light on the fact that these aspects of you were never really parts of you at all—you simply became them unconsciously in the moment. Whether we feel lack, are triggered, or our energies are hijacked by others, we can be drawn into the drama, manipulation or toxic projections attached to it. We can at times become the very thing we are trying to avoid. It takes courage to step outside the norm, see the big picture, allow change or say how you feel and reveal your own vulnerabilities. Speaking authentically from your heart allows you to be heard and seen for who you truly are. There is no ego, no pushiness, no angst expressed or felt within you. You can simply express yourself freely and truthfully.

There's a story that tells of a little girl at her first sleepover. She was feeling a bit reluctant as she was scared to be away from her parents overnight for the first time. There was another girl attending as well, who was excited to go and had slept over before. In the middle of the night, the little girl who was scared awoke and started crying, wanting to go home. So, her parents were called and they came to pick her up.

I believe that there are two different perceptions of the little girl that can come from this story. The first is that she was a baby for not staying, or perhaps that she needs to grow up a bit before her next sleepover. Unconsciously her parents or peers might convey that to her, not realizing or aware that they may be instilling a sense of inadequacy, guilt or shame in her by doing so. The second perception is to see the little girl as courageous and brave for asking for what she needed in the moment. She took care of herself and her needs by doing so. She did not allow fear to take over with thoughts of what was expected of her in staying all night or how she would be perceived by others as a result of her actions. I believe this little girl's decision was an act of self-love.

We place so many expectations on ourselves, and when things do not turn out the way we thought they would, we can feel disheartened or upset. Holding onto these negative feelings can then open up a whole realm of other thoughts and worries. This can all occur in our minds without realizing it, and each thought can potentially build a sense of fear within ourselves until we feel the need to avoid or hide the truth of our feelings.

Here are two scenarios that can shine light on how we might create such situations for ourselves:

- The first is having a baby—one of the most beautiful and amazing blessings you can experience in life. You read all the books, you talk to your own mom, you talk to other moms and picture the love you will undoubtedly feel for your newborn child when he or she arrives. You picture your family happy as you engage with your little one as they grow. Then, the baby arrives and everything does not feel quite as perfect as you expected. Although you love your new bundle, at the same time fear begins to creep in as you begin to realize that you don't have all the answers, and this fills you with doubt about your abilities as a mom. Perhaps you've thought about how great it would be to stay home after your child's birth and how happy you would be. Yet, when you arrive home, you find the transition from once working and feeling in control of your life, to your new world of sleepless nights and diapers, chaotic. It may leave you missing how things used to be, which may lead you to feel guilty or ashamed, because you think, *I'm supposed to be happy, right?* So, *OMG, I'm a terrible mom!* These are the feelings you can internalize and choose not to share for fear of how you will be perceived by others. Shame may arise as the feeling of inadequacy enters your thoughts, resulting in even more ruminating and self-sabotaging. The truth is that vulnerability takes courage and shows strength. Accepting and expressing openly who you are, where you are and what your reality is in the moment allows you to be seen, heard and loved not only by others, but by yourself. So, choose a person who allows this for you, one who is willing and worthy of hearing your story, and share it.

- The next scenario is retirement—something we all dream of and can't wait for. You work hard, plan and save for it expecting it to be the most wonderful time of your life, whether you choose to enjoy your time with your family, grandchildren or perhaps travelling the world. You expect it all to be wonderful and feel amazing. Then you get there and perhaps find that things are not quite as you had planned or thought. Perhaps you don't have the money you had hoped for, or maybe you now have health limitations or restrictions or, on the upside, maybe everything did all work out and yet you still somehow feel disappointed by how it actually seems to feel when you arrive. You expected that it would all be different than it actually is. Do you ever wonder why that is? Become curious and ask yourself, "What is stopping me from accepting my reality as it is or where I am?" What stories are you telling yourself? Why do you "think" you need it to be different or more?

Both of these scenarios are different in nature, yet can leave us feeling the same way. In both, we have perceived and expected ourselves to be a certain way or expected things will play out in our lives a certain way before we got there. We set these thoughts in our minds, believing and expecting them to bring us joy, placing our happiness outside of ourselves and leaving it to the unknown of the future.

When something is not as we had intended or thought it would be, we can feel let down, upset or like we must be doing something wrong. This may lead us to compare our lives or ourselves to others, intensifying the feeling of lack already within. We are unable to see that although things may be different than expected, it is OK, and we are OK. Negative thoughts keep us from seeing, accepting and enjoying where we are and what is. They are the very things that limit our ability to embrace the blessings that are around us in the present moment. The truth is, it's really not the situation that is upsetting us, it is our thoughts, expectations and perceptions, along with the resistance we feel to it all that is actually creating our upset. We may not like what is happening, but we can learn to accept and embrace where we find ourselves and instead choose to shift our thoughts towards a more positive outcome by taking a few slow deep breaths and asking ourselves, "OK, this is my reality or where I am now, what is my best option to move forward?" This brings you back to the present and allows you to choose with more clarity.

When you find yourself in a disappointing situation, ask yourself the following few questions:

Why do I feel this way? What story am I telling myself? What are my expectations, thoughts or beliefs around what is happening and where do they come from? Are they helping me or limiting me to access the joy, love or peace I desire?

Become curious about yourself and be truthful, yet loving to what arises. Whatever energy comes up? Feel it fully and then let it pass through you without judgment, if possible. Tell yourself the truth around your perceived story: "I am doing the best I can." "I have so much to be grateful for." "I love myself, and I love my life!" Changing the story you tell yourself and finding the blessings and gratitude in it changes how you view, love and show up in the world. How? Feeling abundance and love within ourselves, and for the blessings we do have today, allows you to shift and view your world through the same eyes. Yes, things may be different than expected or what you thought would happen, yet can you find the blessings you have in your new reality? Though they are plentiful, they are often not easily seen outwardly when we are in a lack mentality. So, open your heart, allow love to fill you from the inside out and watch how your view of yourself, your life or the world changes before your eyes.

It's Not Really About You

One of the biggest perceptions I believe most of us have that has the potential to hurt us is thinking that everything that happens to us and around us is somehow about us. When a family member, friend or spouse seems to take their frustrations out on us or disregard us, or if they don't quite live up to our own expectations, it can feel very personal. Questions like, "What did I do wrong?" or, "How could they do that to me?" might run through our minds. We expect a certain reaction from them and then feel hurt or unjustly treated when things turn out differently. This can land especially hard when we do something for someone expecting to be validated or loved back, but then find that these feelings are not reciprocated the way we thought they "*should be*". Remember, this all happens in seconds: we get a thought ("Why did they do this?"), our bodies fill with the sensation of that thought (contraction, tightness) and then the story begins in our minds ("They don't love me," or perhaps, "How could they do that to me?"), and it can all quickly become about us. Their actions trigger us; our old beliefs, patterns and inner wounds kick in, and we become immersed in our own stories around them.

This immersion can then play out in a few ways:

- You may find yourself *ruminating*—heading down the rabbit hole, consumed in your thoughts and stories, unable to stop the cycle—as your mind tries to make sense of what has happened. Ruminating has absolutely been a pattern of mine throughout my life. I could always feel my mind swirling, yet at the same time, was totally unaware of how or why it was happening or how to stop it. The truth is, the moment something occurs, it is in the past. We only keep things alive in our minds by retelling the stories or trying to change what actually occurred to what we desire it to be. Ruminating is usually driven by the ego. It doesn't allow you to be present, to be conscious or to see the truth, as presence is simply not out there in all the possibilities and outcomes you are conjuring up in your mind. Becoming aware of this pattern of thought is the first step. Being able to connect the feeling in your body associated with ruminating before the stories in your mind begin is the optimum goal, however, being gentle and patient with yourself is required to get there. Remember, ruminating is a pattern that may show up involuntarily as part of a coping mechanism. When you find yourself spiralling downwards with heavy emotion and your mind is consumed, try to just stop for a moment, if possible, and notice it, breathe slowly and deeply and then ask yourself, "What am I thinking? Is it true?" It can feel unsettling when we become aware of our own internal dialogue and realize how we may be putting our own spin or story into it. That's OK. Just notice, without judgment if possible. Then, take a moment to acknowledge the truth: "Yes, there may be things happening around me or to me, but the reality is that at this moment, I am here and I am OK!" Or you could connect with your surroundings and as example say, "The truth is that right now I am sitting on my couch, warm and safe. I have everything I need." Breathe and allow yourself to feel the calmness in your body as the heavy emotions melt away, and you feel safe. This is your now!

Keeping your mind where your body is allows presence in, and although your outer situation may still be there to deal with, you will know that at that moment, you are really OK. As you begin to connect your thoughts with how you feel, you will gain an understanding of how we create and how we also hold ourselves back with our own limited beliefs. This is awareness!

- I now know that feelings of hurt, sadness or anger are connected to each other, because underneath anger is always sadness that is not being expressed. Any unexpressed fear that you hold inside has the potential to yield the same result. As this buildup of stuck energy rises and comes out, you may find that you react harshly or have strong responses at times and not understand why. For myself, I now understand that fear was a dominant contributor to how I could show up or respond. In the past, although I was able to see and feel the discord that I projected, I did not understand it or why it was there. Thankfully, I do now!

It's simple. We are all energetic beings and attract the energy that we embody back to us. When we hold in any negative feelings, such as hurt, anger or perhaps resentment, they remain in us and become stuck until they are released. So become the energy you wish to attract more of by accepting, releasing and forgiving the past, others and yourself. This will raise your vibration and you will ultimately feel more joy, ease and contentment as a result.

- You may simply *avoid* the situation or walk away. It can feel easier to sometimes use avoidance rather than to tackle something head on. This was something I could do, instead of telling someone how I was really feeling about their actions or words towards me because I feared the possibility of their response. I would instead tell myself they didn't mean what they'd said, or that what they'd done to me was OK, even when it wasn't, and totally disregard my own feelings.

I would tell myself that I was simply giving them the benefit of the doubt and therefore keeping the peace. I can now see that peace was something that I always longed for in my life. I was continually trying to fix things from the outside, to somehow control the outcomes and keep my world feeling happy. I was totally unaware that what I really needed was to look inside and ask myself, "Why am I really scared to show my true feelings?" "What part of me doesn't believe I am worthy of being heard or seen?"

Avoidance is a coping pattern, and one most people use as they believe, like I did, that it was easiest. Yet, I can now see the truth of how the negative energy stayed in me each time it occurred, building up, so that I would eventually end up freaking out over something that seemed like nothing to everyone else, yet was huge to me, and as a result I would be perceived as someone I really wasn't.

The truth is that avoidance does not eliminate problems—it masks them. The negative energy we embody as a result of not showing our true selves, or how we are really feeling, will then attract more of the same energies to us. We may try and show the world a different side of us, but we will not feel ourselves doing it. The unease, discomfort or sense of lack will show up until you look at the hidden pain or wound. The universe will give you ample opportunities, situations and people to help you learn how to stop and notice why you feel the need to avoid something or why you choose not to be seen, so it may be healed.

For myself, looking at the truth of why and how ruminating, feeling hurt and avoiding became a part of me allowed me to then release the energy of them so that I could begin to speak and show up more truthfully, lovingly and authentically.

Releasing Resistance

The truth is, though we expect a lot from ourselves, we also can expect a lot from the other people in our lives. Our spouses, children or other family members may be expected to act or be a certain way, to follow family protocols and to keep traditions going. We somehow expect them to make us happy, and when they can't or don't comply, we then blame them for our perceived unhappiness. We think everyone else has to change or be different, or do what we think is right, unaware that our thoughts, limited beliefs and family patterns are at the bottom of our dismay. Consider this: if you need everyone else to change so that you can be happy, at what point do you look at yourself? Can everyone else *always* be at the heart of your upset? Are you giving your power away to others and then blaming them for taking it?

By becoming aware of your own energy and allowing yourself to feel how you are truly feeling, you can connect more deeply with yourself, and you can then look at your negative feelings with curiosity. This will begin to uncover the many layers that may have accumulated within you over the years. As you peel back each layer and see what's inside, you will gain a sense of control within yourself, and you will begin to reveal how you have been giving your power away.

We have all adopted our own ways of being and our own beliefs of how to do things and how to view the world. When someone says or does something that is not in alignment with your beliefs, you may perceive it as wrong, and you may perceive that they are going against you somehow. In those moments, ask yourself, why do I think they are wrong? Why do I think they have to change or do things my way? What are my expectations and perceptions? Where did these beliefs come from? How do I feel as a result?

Not allowing people to be who they are without judgment or expectations is resisting "what is" and is at the heart of most family events that go awry. It can end up being what a lot of people tend to argue over. "I'm doing everything," or "We have always done it this way in the past," or, "What's wrong with them, why are they so difficult to get along with?" These may be a small example of family situations that can arise. It can feel easier to cast blame on or judge others rather than to become curious and look at why we feel the need for them to be different in order for us to be happy, and how *we* are actually allowing their actions to affect us, by resisting them. When we resist or push against others' actions, beliefs or thoughts, there is usually a hidden wound or sense of lack that we are subconsciously carrying. For example, if you find yourself judging others—or thinking *why do I always have to do everything and they don't?*—consider this: Is the other person's laziness, that you believe, really the truth of your unhappiness OR is there possibly resentment within you, wishing you could relax more too? And if so, why is it there? What is underneath the resentment you feel? Why can you not allow yourself to relax? That, my friend, is the golden nugget to seek!

A few years ago, I had the privilege of meeting a lovely and highly spiritual woman through a mutual friend. She told me something that shifted how I see things. She began telling me about a woman who was complaining to her about how her husband has to always be right and how incredibly frustrating it was to her. The woman then simply smiled at me and ended her story there as if it was the end of the story. I didn't get it. What was the point of the story? What did she mean? I asked her, "Then what?"

She smiled at me and said simply that the woman complaining wasn't able to see that she was the same as her husband. And again, that was it, with no explanation of why, which I now see was her way of teaching me, for I would have to understand the hidden meaning myself. "Hmm," I nodded as though I had understood, yet I would have to think about this for a minute.

When we consider someone else to be pushy or having to be right, we often feel justified by our own actions because, after all, they are the ones being pushy, not us, right? When in fact, if we are triggered or have any kind of negative reaction that makes us feel the need to push back, we indeed become the same as them. Why? Because we too are resisting "what is," meaning we are pushing against their thoughts, by asserting our way, our thoughts, beliefs or expectations. We are wanting something to be different than it is. Resistance of any kind simply means the ego is attached to you thereby leaving you feeling like you need to prove or justify your thoughts back. If you could, at that moment, instead take a step back to gain clarity, you'd begin to see the unconscious nature that is being displayed by the other person, and perhaps by yourself. Is your reaction getting you closer or further away from your intended desire? What is behind or underneath the need to feel right? How would you feel if you let the other person simply have their opinions? Could you? If not, do you know why?

It is when we are able to become present, conscious and loving to ourselves, that we can then hear the words of others without ego. This means their words don't land on us—there is no attachment and therefore no reaction. We are able to stand in our truth, unscathed by the other person, knowing that we are separate and enough just as we are. The truth is, you are very much separate from and not defined by anyone or anything. You are beautiful and uniquely you, and you have nothing to prove. This truth can be achieved as the ego slowly loses its hold on you. For as it's released, you will begin to feel the power within, which will in turn strengthen your connection to your higher self.

> *Self-control is strength. Calmness is mastery.*
> *You have to get to a point where*
> *your mood doesn't shift*
> *based on the insignificant actions*
> *of someone else.*
> *Don't allow others to control*
> *the direction of your life.*
> *Don't allow your emotions*
> *to overpower your intelligence.*
>
> —MORGAN FREEMAN

Chapter 6

INTERLUDE

Choosing From The Heart

On a more personal note of how I can relate to and have experienced these things (perception, expectation and resistance) is when the time came during my divorce to decide whether or not I would live in or sell the family home. I had been living in it alone for about a year as we settled everything. The memories of the last twenty years that we had lived there were etched into every room, and it felt like I would be losing a part of myself and my life by selling it. There was a constant battle inside of me each day, as I went back and forth continually in my mind asking myself: "How do I leave? But how can I stay?"

The memories, although beautiful for the most part, were the exact reason I felt I should move. They were everywhere and kept me in the past, missing what I thought was. I needed a new view to be able to move forward, so I began in search of a new home. I had no idea what kind of home I wanted, where to look or whether to rent or buy. There were too many options for my brain at the time. So, I looked at everything, both newer and older. I remember walking into a beautiful new place thinking, "Maybe I could live here," yet I found the decision so hard. Nothing felt like home to me. When you feel you were happy where you were, your mind will find many reasons to avoid changing to something new. It will bring up all sorts of doubts and fears that keep you from signing on the dotted line. I can now see that leaving my home was reinforcing to me, in no uncertain terms, that my home and the life that I had known for so long, was indeed no more, and this was a reality that I found difficult to accept or even acknowledge at the time, even though it was happening. In over a year's time, everything that had been my life was becoming dismantled, piece by piece, and I felt like I had no control over anything!

With the house now sold, I was feeling overwhelmingly frustrated in trying to find somewhere to move to. I felt very alone, with no place to call my own, and moving day was inevitable and becoming closer each day. I decided to move in with my mom and continue my search from there.

I was so thankful she offered her place to me, yet I also found that it brought up more feelings of resistance in me. Moving in with my mom at fifty-six was not what I had expected or thought would ever be happening for myself. I had envisioned and expected my life to be different. It was truly a humbling experience.

I would often sit in my bedroom in my mother's house with my laptop in hand, listening for countless hours to all sorts of meditations and YouTube videos about how to release anxiety and fear while also striving to become more present and mindful. I found my mom's big deep bathtub to be a godsend, and it became my sanctuary. I would run a warm bubble bath and light beautifully scented candles and place them all around the room. While soaking, I would listen softly to self-love and "I am worthy" affirmations and repeat them to myself as I lay in the warm, soothing water.

Sometimes, it's hard to find the good in what is perceived to be bad. When I moved to my mom's, I was in a state of deep despair, grief and victim hood, feeling the loss of my marriage and family home. But now, I can see the blessings of spending the six months I did with her. That time was a gentle path towards living on my own, and I found that once I was able to surrender to my new reality, it became much easier. Surrendering means letting go of resistance and accepting what is. The truth was, I was able to sit in my room by myself when I needed to, all the while knowing and feeling the energy that surrounded me, which was one of love and caring. I was safe. The conversations I shared with my mom were deepened and enriched by my raw emotions, which left us feeling closer. The beautiful park by her place was where I found stillness.

After living with my mom for a couple of months, my panicky feelings about finding my new home began to subside. I knew I would find one when the time was right. Then, one day, seemingly out of nowhere, I found it—or in truth, it found me. When I walked in the door, I just knew. Everything from the beautiful young couple renting it to the amazingly beautiful view that surrounded it felt right. It was perfect and peaceful. I had found my new home!

When moving day arrived, I felt excited and yet surprised to feel resistance building up also. I really didn't understand why it was happening at the time, but the truth was, I was leaving a place where I felt safe to go to yet another new place, but totally alone this time. It felt a bit unnerving to be honest, which might sound silly, but it was not until then that I realized, holy cow, I've never lived on my own before! Making the move, I found was a gradual one. I slowly transferred my belongings from my mom's to my new home, yet could not totally move there myself. I can now see that I was resisting my new life. When I finally moved in, I vividly remember the feeling that washed over me as I sat on my beautiful new couch, looking at what I can only describe as empty space. Even though it was fully furnished, it felt empty and loneliness was invading every part of me. I had purposefully surrounded myself with soft blankets, loving sayings and homey-feeling things, yet I could not see them anywhere. As I sat on my couch night after night for the next couple of weeks, tears once again flowed like the raging waterfall I had felt a few years before. The beauty and peacefulness that I thought I had found, eluded me!

What now? Is this my life? This was the strong narrative in my mind. I felt like I had taken two steps backwards, from just beginning to find a sense of ease at my mom's to anxiety and sadness again. This was the story I told myself for a bit, until one day, I felt a shift in myself, and I remember saying to myself, "Okay, Bevy, this is your new home. What now?" I believe wholeheartedly that my true healing began in that moment, and a few days later, I stated this intention out loud: "It's time! I am now going to love myself the way I loved my family for all those years—unconditionally!"

My divorce was finalized, and I was beginning to slowly figure out who I was and what my life could potentially look like moving forward. I remember sitting at the island in my kitchen one morning, scanning through jobs and other possible things I could now do, feeling the stress of having to figure it all out. I did still have a casual job at the time, but I didn't think it was enough. My perception of who I was had been erased with my marriage, *I thought*, and I was desperate to find my purpose and worth, thinking I needed to make more money to prove myself worthy and then I would find it. The self-sabotaging thoughts (*They'll never hire you! You're too old!*) were running rampant and creating havoc within me. As I sat there scrolling the various possibilities of jobs that I could apply for day after day, my anxiety and fear rose more with every potential job I came across. Even though I would think they sounded interesting, I found that I could not bring myself to hit the send button to actually apply. It was like the devil and angel once again debating inside of me. My mind (devil) was telling me all the reasons I wouldn't be OK if I didn't apply, and my soul (angel) was lovingly nudging me and showing me the true path to take—towards choosing to heal myself.

I have come to understand that I was desperately trying to become something I thought I "should" be—to become what society perceived as right or respectable—and I was not accepting where or who I was at the time. I was worried about what other people would think of me because not only was I divorced, but I was also alone and without the status of a "real" job. In my eyes, I was not enough as I was. Therefore, I was continually trying to force the square peg into the round hole, feeling frustrated when it wouldn't fit. I was trying to make my life and myself into something it wasn't, which simply is not possible to do. Once I allowed this awareness in, I was able to ask myself, "What do I really need at this moment?"

The truth was, I had just been through a painful couple of years, and what I really needed was time.

When I allowed myself to listen to what my body was telling me, and closed my laptop and let all of those thoughts go, the anxiety I felt began to subside. It became clearer to me that I was indeed creating the frustration and anxiety I felt in my mind and body with all the stories I was telling myself about why I needed a different job and why I needed to be better than I was. I can see now that the nudge to resist hitting apply was my soul or intuition asking me to see and choose differently—to choose *ME*.

Our inner guidance is always leading us, and we always have a choice whether to listen to it or not. There is no doubt in my mind that I chose the path of least resistance, even though ironically, it did not feel that way initially. There are times when feeling resistance is the sign needed to illuminate the best path that we are otherwise unable to see for ourselves. Closing my laptop gave me the time I needed to heal, grow and learn to love and accept myself in the following months. And that process has been instrumental to me in creating the life I truly wanted.

> *As you start to walk on the way, the way appears*
>
> —RUMI

Chapter 7
The Eyes of Illusion

Who We Become

Our true reality is that we are all spiritual beings, in a human body, having a human experience. At our core, we embody the essences of love, light and harmony. We are all connected to each other and to the universe, and we are all divinely guided along our life paths.

Illusion is a false idea or belief, a deceptive appearance or impression. When in an unconscious state, we may see illusion as reality, yet when the light of consciousness shines on it, it cannot be denied or unseen for what it is.

One of the hardest things in life is letting go of something
YOU THOUGHT WAS REAL.

—UNKNOWN

The stories we tell ourselves, our beliefs, patterns, roles we engage in and the fear around it all can affect how we perceive our reality. Yes, the people in our lives and our experiences are there to help us grow and evolve, and they teach us along the way. However, we can sometimes create our own illusions of these things, particularly when we believe everything and everyone around us is real and only allow ourselves to see what we want to see or when we resist seeing that things have somehow changed. When this happens, we may become someone different ourselves. For example, if we have a strong desire to fit into a situation or with someone, we may begin to lose sight of who we really are, thinking we "should" be or react a certain way. When we do these things, we are not following our internal guidance, but instead choosing to do what is easy and what allows us to feel loved or safe (or so we think). When repeated, these actions can become our beliefs and alter how we perceive our lives, ourselves and others. It can slowly become our version of reality.

However, as your awareness strengthens, you may begin to see things through a clearer lens. As you become more conscious, you will also be able to spot the unconscious nature in others more easily. The unconsciousness of others doesn't make them wrong or bad; it's simply who they are or who they think have to be at that time. As you become aware of this, you will gain clarity and understanding of how we all create from where we are on our own journeys. Remember, most people project the parts of themselves that they want to show the world, and it can be very disillusioning to become aware that someone is not who or what you thought they were. Equally, you may experience this in yourself as you realize that you are not really who you thought you were also. Unconsciously, and for the most part unintentionally, we all "become" someone else at some point as we navigate life. However, over time we can then believe that this false sense of us is who we are, and it can feel quite unsettling when our true self starts to reveal itself. The roles, stories and patterns that have followed us in our lives are how we perceived, thought and believed we were and who we are. Yet, as you connect to your inner self, you will begin to realize that you are so much more. Although you can choose not to look at it, believe it or want it, you simply cannot deny it.

Our Blurred Vision

The roles we portray in our lives create a sense of who we are in our minds, and we can literally change ourselves to become the best version of these roles to fit in or to be liked or loved. We believe this gives us a sense of worth, connection and purpose in life. When asked, we proudly say, "I'm a CEO," or "I live in this beautiful area, have a wonderful family, two dogs and a cat." Life is perfect and we always seem to be fine! You get the picture. But is it really true? Are we always fine? Why do we *need* to be or perceived that way? And who are we without it all?

Our longing for love, acceptance and validation can feel incredibly strong when we carry a sense of lack or unworthiness inside ourselves. So, what happens then when we want or "need" more love, stability or happiness in our lives? We keep searching for it. We tell ourselves we will be happy when this or that happens or doesn't happen—"Perhaps when I make more money… find the right guy… have a baby… or retire." By thinking this, we are missing out on the now and the blessings we do have, instead dreaming about what will be in the future and living with a feeling of continual lack. We have perhaps attached our worthiness and happiness to everything out there—material possessions, statuses we've acquired and how we measure up to it all. *We think* these things *define us.*

Longing for happiness from outside yourself can lead some people to choose to suddenly leave their homes, to move and start anew. Some leave their relationships, blaming their partners for their unhappiness. Some people continually buy new material possessions, perhaps trying to keep up with their friends or neighbours. We think, believe and tell ourselves that all of these things will make us happy. And yes, they might for a while. Yet, it is these decisions that will undoubtedly leave you continually searching.

The truth is that happiness really is an inside job. It is felt within, and it's an illusion of sorts to think that it's out there somewhere in an exotic country, in other people or in our possessions. That's why we may sometimes feel unhappy again a short time after our big purchase, moving or leaving or changing relationships.

In the end, we are still there... *UNCHANGED.*

Everyone loves to have nice things in their lives, and everyone is deserving of having them. Yet, it is only when we are aligned with our higher selves that we are able to truly enjoy them. For it is then that we see them differently, without attachment. We no longer need them to define or validate us, and we feel happy and secure whether we have them or not. They are simply seen more as a blessing, rather than needs. With patience, practice and dedication to yourself and your journey, you too will come to understand and integrate this truth. You are always enough, simply because you are here! You are not what someone tells you that you are, your value does not come from your possessions, nor are you a part of the happenings around you. It's all an illusion! Awakening your heart and soul brings awareness to the truth of your existence. You will begin to see, feel and know that you are indeed enough as you are, and separate from it all. This then opens the door for you to feel joy and contentment in the small or seemingly simpler things in life. Your blessings will become more abundant, not because you necessarily have more, but because you see and feel them in everything.

Each step of my journey through and past the divorce has brought new awareness to me. Not only awareness about myself, but also about others and how I was perceiving life as I knew it. I became increasingly aware of how I was giving my own power away by defining my own worth by everyone and everything out there. The following is an example of an illusion I had created in my mind. Once it came to light, I was guided through the steps of understanding and healing it.

In the beginning, when I was knee-deep in tears and trying to make sense of the pending divorce, I began seeing a therapist, telling her all my woes and how I could not give up on my marriage. After a couple of sessions, she asked me the question, "What marriage?" I stopped and glared at her with confused, water-filled eyes. "What? My beautiful marriage, weren't you listening?" She replied by asking me, "Is that the truth now?" Again… What?? It was at that very moment that I remember feeling this huge rush flow over me, and it was as if a light bulb had been switched on. It was in that moment that it hit me, as I realized no, it was not at all my reality. Instead, it was what I wanted to still be true and was the story, or illusion, I was telling myself. The truth was, my husband was already gone—not physically, but he had made his decision—yet, the story in my mind remained as what I had always believed was real. Therefore, my mind could not make sense of what was really occurring, and it would not allow the actual truth to settle in me. I believe it did this as protection. For if I had let the truth in right away, all the feelings of unworthiness and the overwhelming sense of being unloved would have invaded my body.

I thought that the end of my marriage would be my fault if I did not fight for it. I thought that I "should" somehow be able to change and fix things, because to me, in my mind, that's what I was good at. My role as mom for all those years had been keeping my whole family safe and happy, fixing and kissing their boo-boos so to speak, and loving them. It's who I was and how I saw myself. If I could not somehow fix this, then in my eyes I would have failed. I would not be enough! This mindset opened the door for shame and guilt to begin manifesting within me, and they engulfed and penetrated every part of my being. I felt immense helplessness, total inadequacy and in deep, deep despair! My life that I had known and who I was in it made no sense to me anymore, and I was left sitting in the disillusionment of it all.

It was through this time in my life that I learned of, "the dark night of the soul", which may be triggered within you when something you considered meaningful in your life suddenly changes or ceases to be, and you can't explain why. The meaning of your life, yourself and who you thought you were suddenly makes no sense. As a result, you are left in a very dark place.

Learning about this concept and how our minds play a role in it, gave me a deeper understanding of what I was experiencing. It allowed me to see that I was not really delusional, which was, quite honestly, sometimes how I had felt. I was beginning to understand that I had literally given my whole self into my marriage and motherhood, and these things had defined me and how I saw myself. I loved my life and believed we were happy. So, when it all ended, to me, who I was ended too. It was like a death of sorts—I was not only mourning the loss of my marriage, but also the loss of myself.

This would become a long, deeply personal, internal process that would weave me through various stages of grief, discovery, lessons and growth. I found that when you are faced with such an experience, the only way to deeply heal is to go through it all. So, I allowed myself the time to experience every step, every emotion and every lesson. It was while I was moving through these steps that I remember being in a particular meditation class and learning about trust and we were asked the questions, "Do we exit?" and "Who were we without our labels or roles?" This was paramount for me to consider at the time, as I had just spent the day cutting up and discarding my personal ID cards and changing my status from married to divorced, so I really dug deep and thought, *OK, who I've been and how I've lived has changed… has been deleted in a sense… but I'm still here.*

So, who am I *really*?

As I sat with this question, I realized that I am more than who I "think" I am, or thought I was in the past. There is more to me than what I can see. I then thought, *Who I was, is only a part of who I truly am.* I could sense and grasp the idea of connecting to *all* of me: my body, my mind and my soul. My inner being!

What I learned was, when you are stripped of who you thought you were, you are left in your rawest form—you are virtually cracked open! This is your opportunity to look inside. This is your opportunity to reveal and feel the true essence of who you are and understand that you really are so much more than you think. In time, I gained space for my mind, heart and soul to expand, to love and awaken to the beauty within, which in turn allowed me to connect with my higher self. A connection that has grown stronger and more deeply within me over time, and one that required compassion, patience and dedication to attain. I am still me—mom, grandma, friend and daughter, that will never change. Only now I am connected to and freely share the love, peace and beauty within. That "I Am!" That we all are!

Only Seeing the Good Does Not Always Create Good

There are many stories we tell ourselves that keep us feeling good during our days: "Everything is always fine," "We are good," "I love my job." All of these may be true at times, but are they always? We tell ourselves everything is good, thereby believing it, and then we unconsciously create from there. When your belief is that everything is always good, it can shield the truth of your reality in your mind. You simply paint the picture you want to be true. Some people say they live in their own bubble and admit to not wanting to acknowledge the truth or know everything, believing this will make them feel better. But does it really? What truth are they living? And what are they really trying to avoid?

Avoiding, denying or resisting your reality does not change it. It only creates a false sense of being okay and allows you to resist healing the part of you that is actually in lack. This is the part of you that is hidden underneath the "need" you feel for you or your life to be seen as good, nice or perfect. Why is it there? We tell ourselves stories to justify our thoughts and actions, not only to ourselves, but with others. And it's true that by doing so, your outer world may look good to both yourself and others, but how is your inner world? Do you often feel uneasy, uncomfortable or stressed and wonder why?

Take a moment and pause to think about how you feel when you or your life are seen as imperfect in some way? Do you become fearful or afraid? And if so, of what? Do you find you judge or justify yourself? Do you feel ashamed or guilty? If so, do you now why? How does it make you feel? It's important to remember that these are just your thoughts and not the truth of who you are. They are from a past belief or pattern that you now hold true, or perhaps there may be a past hurt attached to your thoughts. Becoming curious about why these thoughts are there and how they make you feel are the first steps. Self-awareness is key and will lead you on the path to healing and releasing them.

Dig deep and ask yourself: Who or what am I defining myself by?

By resisting our reality or by not allowing ourselves and others to just *be* who we all are, we only intensify our own sense of lack and add undo stress or anxiety to ourselves. You may choose to avoid yourself or your reality, yet the loving energy of who you truly are remains in you, wanting to be seen and felt. Thus, you feel unease each time you are striving to become someone you are not, or when you only see the "good" parts of someone or something, avoiding the truth. This feeling is there to show you that you are out of alignment. It shines a light on your resistance to being authentic and why you instead feel you need to be something you are not. Remember, we are always enough just as we are, no exceptions. Unfortunately, we can't always sense this and therefore may be left trying to change ourselves or our reality. When this happens, we may feel out of control within ourselves. We may unconsciously, or at times intentionally, begin to try to control our lives, ourselves and others by manipulating them.

Manipulation is simply creating a skewed vision or an illusion of something. It may be something you learned how to do when you were young as a way of getting what you wanted or needed. It may also be a coping tool to allow ourselves to shine or be seen the way we want to be, yet cannot show authentically. If you remain unconscious, manipulation may slowly become a pattern, a way of avoiding the real hurt or pain inside, as it gives you a false sense of control over yourself. It can make you feel or be perceived as superior. I have witnessed people become chameleon-like, changing themselves or only showing certain aspects of themselves to fit into a given situation. They become who "they need to be", so they will be accepted, validated or liked by others. Whether you unconsciously or intentionally change yourself, you only keep the illusion going and the wounds you embody hidden. In time though, the reality of it all will begin to shine through.

As you gain self-awareness, you may discover several things; that you have been manipulated in the past, you may have witnessed others' chameleon-like behaviours and allowed them or you may realize that you have manipulated others yourself to achieve what you needed in the past. Try not to be too hard on yourself if any of these are brought to your awareness, as it can feel unsettling as you begin to notice who you were or what you allowed in your life. Remember, these things most likely occurred unconsciously, and when we are unaware, we simply don't notice until after the fact. These may be the times when we found ourselves doing something we really didn't want to do, or maybe found ourselves scratching our heads because a story we were told by someone completely changes when you are both with other people, and you are left feeling confused, yet you know what you heard originally. Both of these things can leave you feeling triggered when you are unconscious, leaving your ego to take over. When the ego is triggered, it can possibly then change who you become or how you react, the more you find yourself engulfed in the skewed story.

Manipulation may be obvious and easy to see in others, or it may be hidden and more covertly exhibited, which can be more difficult to recognize. In any case, when you are deeply connected to someone, whether through family, friendship or a romantic relationship, it can feel very unsettling when you begin to notice that something is off. And, if your pattern has also been one of avoidance and only seeing the good in others, then you may find that you feel stuck and unsure of what the truth is. This is because you want to believe that this person is one way, yet at times you can clearly see another side emerge. This confusion, although frustrating, is actually a good thing. This is a sign that your awareness is opening and allowing you to begin breaking through the illusion or untruth that's being displayed. This may also be the time when your mind (the ego) will try to keep you safe by denying it. However, being able to calm the mind and then take steps to become more present and conscious is when clarity and truth will prevail.

If you are not ready to accept "what is"—whether that is seeing yourself, others or a situation in a different light, it can feel overwhelming or uncomfortable to see the truth. Initially, you may simply push it back down and try to maintain your usual way of life, by giving others or yourself the benefit of the doubt, and that's perfectly OK too. But the thing is, you cannot unsee the truth, once seen. You always have a choice though. You can either look the other way, stay the victim and blame others for their perceived unjust actions, making them the bad guys, or you can choose to say, "OK, yes, this did happen" or "They did do this," but then also ask yourself, "Who was I," "What did I allow or avoid?" and "Why?" Take responsibility for yourself and your role in the situation, as we only really have control over ourselves. We cannot control the situation itself or the people we find ourselves in it with. And although we can't change who we were, we can change who we are now and who we will be moving forward! This is how we redeem our own inner power!

As for me, I knew I was ready! I needed to understand why and how certain events occurred throughout my life and how I didn't see them or why I chose not to see them. What was I afraid of? Or what was I gaining by allowing them? This too was a deeply personal healing. At first, as I began looking at myself and others, I just allowed myself to feel. I let myself express and release all the hurt and anger that came up, both for myself and towards others, without resistance. I then began clearing the stuck negative energy with meditation, affirmations and by bringing stillness into my days. This process opened up space to bring more clarity, awareness and understanding to the forefront. I was then able to turn my focus away from the perceived deeds of others and place it back onto myself. Seeing with conscious awareness, taking responsibility for who I was at that time and forgiving and loving those aspects of myself.

The truth is, in the past, I loved to please others. I believed in my heart that the people in my life were being honest with me in their shown actions. I can now see that I did this to a fault at times, taking most people at their word and believing it all as truth. In reflection, I also see that my level of awareness was already elevated back then, even though I didn't know it. For as certain situations occurred throughout my life, I recall feeling uneasy inside. My body and intuition were always sending me signals, but I could not or did not want to hear or see them (I believe a little of both), instead choosing to push the uneasiness back down, remaining unconscious and unhealed.

I have also come to understand that our mind and body will only take in whatever we are ready to look at, and the truth will only be revealed to us when we are ready to see it with clarity. No, we may not like the truth or be ready for the associated hurt or pain that comes along with it, but our heart and soul knows we are ready to grow from it all. And when we are willing to trust and allow it to all unfold, the universe leads the way!

Remember, to always be patient and gentle with yourself as you go through this process. Life is a journey, not a race. Healing is a deeply personal gift you can give yourself. Things can take time to unravel. Seeing your choices of the past with love allows you to release, shift or change them with more ease, which will then illuminate what you truly desire moving forward. The more you align with this higher energy, the clearer your path becomes.

Chapter 8
People Pleasing

Is It Really Love?

Do you ever wonder why you can sometimes feel compelled to be everything to everyone, or why you feel like you have to do things that you really don't want to, or why you neglect your own needs, thinking you will somehow look better because of it?

This was me in a nutshell, and the story I told myself around it was, "That's just who I am. I'm a people pleaser." I honestly thought this was a good thing and actually felt a sense of pride because of it at times. The definition of love for me was "making others happy." I had always felt better giving than receiving and can now see how I would diminish myself and my sense of worth in the process.

From childhood, I was taught that it's better to give and that to receive was somehow selfish. This pattern of belief allowed guilt and other insecurities to rise in me when faced with receiving love or help from others, as my inner self would feel I was selfish or not worthy or deserving of these offerings. Yet, I would feel a sense of pride and joy when giving my love or help to others, which is how these feeling manifested into people pleasing. They felt better! Everything I've come to learn about why I was like this has become invaluable to me. I am now able to see that my behaviour simply developed from the era in which I grew up in, mixed with the beliefs and patterns of who I thought I should be, or had to be, in order to be accepted and loved.

Honestly, looking back at the years of my marriage, I do recognize that I felt anxious and frustrated about trying to be and do it all. It made me feel crazy at times, yet I felt it was the "right" way to be. In my eyes, it was just what you did and what was expected. So I forged forward, totally unaware and unconscious of how and what I was creating along the way, both in myself and with others. I loved the rush I felt when others were happy. I felt worthy, needed and loved by them. I based my happiness on the expectations and outcomes of others, which I now know is not sustainable. Eventually, I slowly began to feel invisible, and

I lost my own inner power and control over myself, having placed it with everyone else. I had showered everyone with love… EXCEPT ME!

I came across the following saying as my self-awareness grew, and when I first read it, I felt the light bulb go off as I could see that it was me and what I had created for myself. I quickly wrote it out and placed it on my fridge as a reminder.

> *The problem with putting everyone else first is YOU'VE taught them you come second.*
>
> —UNKNOWN

There are times when we go the extra mile to help or when we do something we really don't want to do in our quest to help out or make someone else happy. It may be going to a family dinner when you'd rather be home relaxing, or it may be helping a friend in need at a time when you too may find yourself consumed by life, yet you help them anyways. When these actions are shared from an authentic, loving place, they feel amazing to all involved. They are the things that contribute to strong and loving relationships. So, what happens to change this beautiful feeling to one of worry, anxiety or fear?

Consider taking some time to examine your thoughts and how you speak them outwardly. Have you ever noticed the words "I should" or "I have to" are the narratives that drive you or that you tell yourself? Many subconscious beliefs that we embody are derived from our younger years. Perhaps you didn't receive the attention you longed for as a child and felt unloved, unworthy or lived in a toxic environment. Or on the flip side, maybe you only received love and attention when you did something nice or helpful for the adults or siblings in your life. All of these situations have the potential to lead you to people pleasing in a quest to receive love back or to feel worthy, and over time, this can unknowingly become a pattern of behaviour. For me, I now realize that I have always craved love, which was not always freely shown or given to me as a child. Being unaware of the hidden hurt I carried inside, I simply told myself that pleasing people was just what I did, and I had no idea what actually lay beneath it.

Pleasing others is actually a loving gesture and simply means we are longing for connection. It allows us to feel love, but we can sometimes be unaware that we are giving from an empty cup ourselves. It's a wonderful attribute to be loving, kind and helpful to people, and when we are conscious, present and give from the heart, it's authentically given. Giving from the heart feels easy and natural, and we expect nothing in return because our own cup is already full. Alternatively, when we are unconscious of our inner wounds or lack, we please others to achieve a desired outcome or to fill a hole inside ourselves, as our cup is not full. For example, say you are planning a family dinner. Initially, you feel like ordering food and keeping things low-key, and yet instead you find yourself orchestrating a full-course meal because you feel like you have to and it's what's expected of you. Another example might be that you are taking on more than your fair share of work at the office, wanting to be liked or to be seen as a team player. We may give and give to our family, friends or our work and are unable to see that it is slowly becoming a one-sided relationship. Behind each of these examples, there may be a hidden desire or need to be seen, appreciated or loved back, and when you do not receive these in return for your efforts, it can leave you feeling upset or possibly even heartbroken. When we give with the expectation of getting something in return, we may be setting ourselves up for disappointment, hurt and upset. By trying to alleviate this upset, we may then try to control or fix things.

People pleasing and feeling the need to be the "fixer" are like two peas in a pod to me. For when you want everything and everyone to be happy, it follows that you then feel the need to create that environment. This however, is virtually impossible to achieve or sustain. Remember, we only have control over ourselves. Despite this, the mind will keep coming up with the many thoughts, ideas, scenarios and reasons for why and how you need to "make" others happy or fix things. The pressure to do so may then escalate within you, and fear, worry or anxiousness may prevail when you realize you cannot achieve these goals as you have no control over how your actions will be perceived by others. On top of that, have you ever stopped to consider what you are actually creating for yourself, both in your inner and outer world by doing this?

In the past, if I heard from a loved one, whether family or friend, and they had a problem or were hurting in some way, I would immediately go into "fix it" mode. My mind would try and figure out what I could do to help or make it better. This is actually a very loving and caring way to be and quite honestly has always come naturally to me. Yet, as I began healing and loving myself, I became aware of one important question that I wasn't able to acknowledge in the past: *Was I always being asked for my help?* This thought was nowhere in my awareness in the past, as I could only feel the desperate feeling inside myself to help or fix it, and I felt very strongly that it was what I had to do. I was putting all this undue pressure and stress on myself, not because I wanted to, but because it was a belief and pattern of who I thought I had to be. As a result, there were times when the love I thought I was showering on others was not always received in the way I intended.

I've come to understand that I am a "sensitive." I am also a highly empathetic woman. This simply means that I not only feel the energy of others easily, but I can also take on their energy as my own. I also, unknowingly could allow my energy field to be hijacked, in a sense by others; thus, the feeling of desperation! I have always led with my heart and felt compassion for others, which is beautiful, yet, in order to be and show that part of me authentically, I would have to heal and release the parts of me that felt I *needed* to be and do that. There is a distinct difference between being loving to others genuinely and being loving because you feel the need to be. When coming from truth, it is given with an open heart and is freely given, and when coming from a "need", it derives from a place of lack and the ego is attached. By achieving this, I would be able to separate myself from the pain of others, while still being loving and compassionate towards them. It would free me from the negative energy of others as it would no longer land on me. I have found that this changed how I experienced situations and people. It has released me from going down the emotional rabbit hole of trying to fix everything and please everyone. I can now instead show up more present, loving, conscious and compassionate—more myself!

I invite you to become curious and honest about where you are giving from. Is it an authentic place? Consider the following questions:

- Do you ever notice that you feel like a martyr? Do you do things you don't really want to do and then blame others for it? And if so, how do you feel as a result?

- Do you give your time and love to everyone except yourself?

- Do you feel like you can't or are unable to give yourself what you need? Do you fail to include yourself in the equation or to set healthy boundaries?

- Are you carrying a subconscious belief that makes you think you have to or should do something to be perceived as a good person, liked or even loved, and now feel stuck in this pattern? Has this pattern now become someone elses expectation of you?

- Take notice: Can you speak openly or do you feel invisible? Are the wants of others overriding yours?

Each of these scenarios has the potential to render you into a sense of powerlessness and, when continued, can slowly become the reality of how you see yourself and live your days.

It's important to remember that:

It's not our job to make someone else happy, instead look inward at why you feel the need to do so.

So, if you begin to realize that any of the above scenarios are how you feel or have been in the past, remain ever gentle and ask yourself these questions:

- Where do these thoughts or actions come from?
- What or who is really telling me I need to be or do these things?
- What is it that I need or lack that is behind these feelings?
- What outcome do I really want or desire? Is what I'm doing creating that for me?
- What small steps can I take now to shift or change in this moment?

I remember throughout my marriage often saying to myself, if my kids and spouse are happy, then I'm happy. And I honestly felt I was. I had no idea about my cup, let alone how to fill it, and believed it was selfish somehow if I did. I was so good at giving love, compliments and compassion to others, and yet I felt uneasy when receiving any of them back.

I was totally unaware of my inner sense of lack and low sense of self-worth that I had been carrying with me until it was brought to light with the dismantling of my marriage. It was truly one of the most difficult things to look at, as I had always only chosen to see the confident and self-assured side of myself. It's easy to see the perceived "good" parts of ourselves, yet it takes courage to look at the other sides. Looking at all aspects of ourselves opens us up to vulnerability, and your true, raw emotions rise up as these other parts are revealed, unveiling the buried pain inside. As mentioned previously, shadow work is essential in healing and transformation, for when we accept, release and forgive ourselves and let go of who we thought we had to be, we become able to accept, trust and love who we truly are! We then have the potential to shift how we love, teach and grow with our loved ones.

Breaking the Cycle

I do believe there is a fine line between being a loving, caring parent and over-giving and wanting to please them and being seen as the "perfect" or perhaps fun parent. Through my years as a stay-at-home mom, I used to find myself walking that line often. As I look back, I am aware that although I could feel and sense the difference when the line was crossed at times, I was not yet self-aware, in that I did not reflect inwardly and question why.

When I was young, before becoming a mom myself, there were two things I used to tell myself: I will always listen to my kids, and I will always make sure my kids know and feel that they are loved, no matter what happens. These intentions were deeply embedded within me, and it was my desire to achieve them as a mom and for my kids to live them out. I can now see that when those intentions were mixed with my own self lack and limited beliefs, it became the perfect concoction for crossing the imaginary line between the unconditional love I undoubtedly felt and, at the same time, creating a somewhat unbalanced relationship with them and with myself.

It can be hard to see the forest for the trees when you are in the midst of child rearing. The hidden fear you carry from the past frames how you perceive, allow or limit yourself in the present. This is then projected onto the ones we love, albeit unconsciously and unknowingly. We believe we are leading with our hearts, as our wish is for our kids to not feel or experience the difficult things we did. Yet, when the fear we carry remains stuck in us, we are unknowingly and for the most part unintentionally, instilling that same fear into them with our actions and words. The fear is all transferable energy, and when it is felt by us, it flows into them.

When our children are young, they need us for survival. We give them food, shelter and love freely and genuinely. As they grow, we may unconsciously allow our role to define us and become engulfed with the need to continue doing this long after it's needed. Although lovingly, we may push our own beliefs onto them in an attempt to "make" them happy or to help them with their problems. If this continues, it can slowly become what we think we need to be and do, and the thoughts of empowering our children can slowly overshadow our own wants and needs. As a result, we may find that we stop showing up for or standing up for ourselves. This is such a fine line because every parent naturally wants good things for their children. The line to me gets crossed when we do this without any awareness of the underlying desire to receive something in return. Maybe it's to feel loved, to prove ourselves or to be seen by our children in a certain way. As our hidden desires grow we begin to try and achieve them. This then involves the ego as we unconsciously begin to show our children that we want for nothing, and therefore, we ask for nothing in return, perhaps thinking they will think we are stronger for it. And although this may be true, let me remind you of how we create our own reality: The problem with putting everyone else first is that *you've* taught them you come second.

By not being a part of the equation and not taking care of your needs, you are not allowing yourself to be seen. When we always portray ourselves as the givers and the fixers for everyone else, we can slowly become or feel invisible. (I know I did.) Meaning, if we stop showing up for ourselves, and as yourself, other people will then stop seeing us. They will come to believe that you are just there for them. They will think that you are always okay and never need anything. Why? Because you've shown them that's who you are. This way of presenting yourself may be derived from your past, and you now think or believe it is the way you are supposed to be. Possibly, this is a family pattern or belief that was passed down to you that you are now unconsciously creating from. Yet, it is one that you have the power to change, if you choose to.

As you gain awareness, both of your surroundings and in yourself, you also gain inner strength. This energy will flow into feeling more in control of your choices in regard to yourself, your children and others moving forward. Although you have no control over your children's choices when they are grown up, you do have control over yours always. You can either continue to be who you "think" or "need" to be with them, or you can choose to become who you are really meant to be. When you choose to show up authentically, at any stage of your life you shine a light for others to follow, learn and grow from and they then will take this knowledge and way of being with them to share as they move along their life path. Thus breaking the cycle and starting anew!

Shifting with the New

One thing that is certain about life is that it always changes, and it's up to you to choose how you will move with it. Rigid thoughts will undoubtedly limit your future, fun and growth, while flowing with ease and embracing the present moment allows you to shift with the new as it appears.

Take a moment one day to look at the outcome of a decision you made to not change your view, your action or your thoughts about a situation or with regards to another person. As a result, how did it end? Are you happy? How were you or others affected? Additionally, consider the scenario from the opposite point of view. Ask yourself these questions:

- What would have happened if I had shifted my thoughts or simply let it be as it was? Would it really have been so bad?

- What are my beliefs or fears about change? Where do they derive from? How do they make me feel as a result?

As things around you change and you stay the same you may be met with a sense of not fitting in, or you may notice that you are always worried instead of being able to join in the fun around you. It's easy to blame others for your unhappiness, yet becoming curious about why you feel this way and understanding how you are actually creating this feeling within yourself will ultimately free you.

Changes within our daily lives and families are inevitable, and we all learn and grow through them—whether you have a family unit that stays together, a divorced family and the blending of two that occurs as a result, or an adoption which brings in new life into an existing family dynamic. In any case, when life changes for any reason, it disrupts the status quo, affecting what you have come to know as the norm. Who we unconsciously or consciously choose to be in those moments not only affects us and the people we love, but it also creates the platform for our future relationships with them.

Today there are many blended and divorced families, and finding the balance in how to give, to love and guide our children can feel nothing short of challenging, especially with all of the varied opinions out there on the "supposed right" way to do it. If you grew up in a family that stayed together and have been taught this is what family does, you may have feelings of confusion, guilt or shame if you now find yourself divorced and are unable to pass on the same family values you learned as a child to your children. You may feel the same if your parenting role has shifted in some way and you are now unable to participate in your children's lives the way you used to. In these cases, your mind may try to tell you that you are not enough now because of these changes. This is one hundred percent false. These feelings of inadequacy are always the result of unhealed pain, beliefs and patterns that we carry.

The truth is, things in your life may have changed; your marital status, where you live now or your time may be more limited with your children, but have you really changed? NO! It is simply your perceptions and your resistance to what is happening that are telling you something is wrong and instilling a sense of fear in you, bringing up emotions that then validate your negative thoughts. And though the change may feel overwhelming, difficult or unwanted, it is the reality you face. So now what? It can take time to navigate and accept the new, yet doing so allows you to release your resistance to it. Seeing it through the eyes of conscious awareness brings a sense of calm, which enables you to see more clearly. You can then notice what you are resisting, expecting or believing "should be" in your mind.

What do you *REALLY* want to create moving forward, and are your thoughts, actions or reactions helping or hindering you? Are you able to see the whole picture?

It's simple: *What you resist, persists!* Why? Because the energy of resistance is carried in you and will therefore attract more of the same negative energy to you. As the end of my marriage was unfolding and in the months that followed, I thought I was somehow helping my relationship with my kids by trying to keep it the same, when the truth was that it was now very different. Learning to accept our new, unwanted reality was not an easy task for any of us. Yet, in time I was able to see that although our circumstances were different, we were still the same. I was still me, and they were still them. I was able to begin to accept and allow everyone involved to be who they were or who they needed to be at that time, and instead set my intentions for how and what I wanted to create for my future with them moving forward. When we become intentional, we create from a place of authenticity and love. It all begins with awareness. I began to realize that there were aspects of myself and how we had all lived in the past that needed to shift in order to become more balanced moving forward. Although, when you desire a change in your life, it's important to remember it begins with you! You create your world, how you will show up and how you will experience it. I was once told that the biggest gift I could give my kids was to love myself. I took that advice to heart and honestly know it to be true. When you love yourself, you no longer feel needy or people please because you are consciously making decisions that envelope all people concerned, *including yourself*. I am now extremely grateful for the abundant love I feel within, for myself and also for the loving relationship I share with my children and family.

Chapter 9

Love Yourself... The Rest Will Follow

*Fall in love with taking care of yourself.
Fall in love with the path of deep healing.
Fall in love with becoming the best version of
yourself but with patience, with compassion and respect to
your own journey.*

—SYLVESTER MCNUTT

Letting It All In

To be honest, the words "self-love" were not in my vocabulary or words I thought about in the past. I believed that putting yourself first meant you were selfish in some way. And yes, I guess for some there may be some truth to that too, if the ego is involved.

SELF-LOVE is actually the foundation of our happiness, health and relationships.

S eeing the

E go allows you to

L et go and

F eel

L ightness of being

O pen heartedness

V ulnerability

E xpansion

Self-love means:

- Accepting who you are and how you got to where you are by taking responsibility for yourself with love, compassion and understanding.

- Allowing yourself to learn and grow from life experiences without judgment of yourself or others.

- Loving and accepting all of yourself (the good, the bad and the ugly) and being willing to change, release or shift what isn't serving you anymore.

- Speaking your truth lovingly and with kindness, yet unapologetically.

- Giving yourself what you need, when you need it, and pampering yourself if needed too. What feels good? Smells good? Fill your own cup!

- Showing others how you want to be treated by giving yourself the love, compassion and respect you desire and deserve. Set healthy boundaries with love.

- Forgiving yourself and others. It's for you and ultimately sets you free.

- Taking responsibility for your life. You have the power to change it and you.

Self-love begins with us and is truly the biggest gift we can give ourselves and then share with others. Have you ever thought or asked yourself, "Do I love myself?" I encourage to try it if you haven't before. Stand in front of a mirror, look at yourself and say the words, "I love you," or "You are beautiful," and notice how you feel. What arises within you? What bodily sensations, feelings or emotions bubble to the surface? These loving words, unfortunately, are not what most people have grown up telling themselves. But why not?

Love is the essence of who we are, and it is eternal. It has no boundaries as the energy of it flows outwardly to others and can be felt from your heart to theirs. As you begin to integrate it and feel the love inside, you eventually become it and ultimately begin to live it. Yet, if this is true, why do we give and share love so freely with others but not with ourselves? If we are all one, connected and made of love, light and harmony, then it stands to reason that we are all worthy of it. The question is: How do we allow it in?

It begins with self-awareness: Who are you really? How do you feel? What do you need? Then picking up a tool that best helps you in that moment, thereby giving yourself what you need. This is the beginning of self-love! It can take the form of a meditation, a walk, a book, reaching out to a trusted friend who allows you to be seen and heard or simply by becoming still, breathing and reaffirming how beautiful you are to yourself. Becoming aware of your needs and being willing to focus on and give them to yourself are essential steps to integrate love within, for you are not able to give yourself what you need if you don't know what that is. So be proud of your willingness to love yourself as you move through each next step.

To find peace within and really love yourself, you first have to get to know the *REAL YOU*. Spend time with yourself. Feel and experience yourself. Connect to your energy, mind, heart, body and soul. Who are you really? What warms your heart? As I moved through these stages, I thought in order to love myself totally, I would have to see all of me. Everything from the inside wounds to the outside body. So, I decided that periodically I would stand naked in front of the mirror for a few moments and look at each part of my body. We all have parts of ourselves that we would like to change or wish were different somehow. My quest, I thought, was to embrace and see myself with love and gratitude for all that I am, including my supposed imperfections. What I found was, as you learn to love all of yourself, and accept who you are, the imperfections start to fade. I don't mean that they are really gone or disappear, but you won't see them in the same way anymore. The negative thoughts of yourself subside, and you begin to feel gratitude within. In fact, I found that after doing this process, I was able to see some of these supposed imperfections parts as beautiful. And when you see and feel beautiful, that energy expands to everything around you.

Seeing the outer and the inner parts of ourselves with conscious awareness can feel uncomfortable and jolt us a bit off balance at first, yet seeing them is imperative to heal them. We cannot heal what we choose to not see or acknowledge. What part of you feels unworthy of love? And why?

Remember that nothing is bad. They are simply parts of you that you deemed not enough. You believed those thoughts and then carried them along with you on your life path, and therefore they can now be released, forgiven and renewed. Willing, allowing and trusting is needed; be willing to look at yourself with an open heart and mind, allow yourself to accept what you see without judgment and trust that you are worthy, enough and lovable just as you are!

Looking back, I can see that everything I needed came to me once I did these things. It was amazing, truly! Whenever I struggled, I always ended up finding exactly what I needed: a book, hearing or seeing a video or coming across a saying or words of wisdom that would guide me towards seeing more clearly. The signs are always there, however, you have to be open and willing to see them and then act on them.

I remember when I was first moving into my condo after staying at my mom's place, I was feeling scared, unsure and resistant to where I was in life. The story I was telling myself in my mind was that I was somehow "less now." I no longer had my house and was unable to see the joy in my new, smaller home. My sense of worth was somehow attached to my house, and I was judging myself by my own perceptions of it changing. Unbeknownst to me, underneath all of these feelings was shame.

One day as I was unpacking my things, one of my dear friends called me. Without thought, I immediately began unloading all of my frustrations onto her. It felt like verbal diarrhea flowing from my mouth—no solid thoughts, just a continuous spewing. Then suddenly in the next moment, I felt like I had had enough and did not want to feel how I felt anymore. I told my friend I'd like to hang up and instead of returning to unpacking, I turned on the TV and saw Brené Brown, who at the time was unknown to me. I sat and listened to her for a moment, and lo and behold she was talking about shame. Brown is an amazing speaker and author, and she was talking about her book, *The Gifts of Imperfection*. I didn't know why, but I quickly wrote down the name of it and bought it the next day. As I read it, I saw myself in her words and remember thinking, "Oh my God, I do that. That's me!" It was super uncomfortable. Yet, I continually found myself in bookstores looking for more of her books, as my longing to become aware of and heal the parts of me that needed my love and attention became stronger as each day passed.

Being open, honest and allowing myself to be vulnerable was huge for me. Vulnerability is indeed a strength, not a weakness. Yet sadly, this is not how it is perceived by most. Our feelings are always valid because they are ours and what make us who we are. So listen to and talk to yourself with love and understanding, like you would a friend. Say "cancel" to any self-sabotaging thoughts or negative expressions, and show compassion to yourself when needed.

·

As I began noticing my own words, it became ever so clear to me that I apologized for everything, even when there was no need to. Learning to undo this habit required me to be aware of each time I did it. I then noticed that the more I spoke authentically, lovingly and with kindness, that there was seldom a need for apologies as I was simply expressing how I truly felt. Remembering that my opinions matter, because I matter. This, I found was something I had to remind myself frequently. I had to remind myself that just because my opinion could be different from that of others, it did not necessarily make them wrong or invalid. If it was spoken without ego attached (meaning without anger, meanness or pushiness behind it), then I was simply being myself, expressing myself and allowing myself to be seen and heard. Being seen and heard were things I now realize I had been trying to be and do most of my life.

Remember, you can't change how others think, what they expect or how they perceive things. Their thoughts are their own and are not to be mistaken with the truth. When you love yourself, you stand in your power, meaning those thoughts projected onto you, no longer land on you. You are simply OK!

Be Strong ... Be Beautiful ... BE YOU

Keeping It Real With Boundaries

Another aspect of self-love is setting healthy boundaries, both for yourself and with others. This can feel uncomfortable or difficult to do at first and may bring up uneasy feelings in you. In a society where people want to be liked by, connected to and validated by others, you may think that expressing your own needs may be seen as selfish or others may not like it or you as a result. Even if this is true, does it mean that you should shy away from implementing them?

The more I got to know myself, the more I found that I was doing just that. I would look the other way, give people the benefit of the doubt or tell myself all the reasons why I couldn't or shouldn't say how I felt. Doing so then brought up all the fears associated with those reasons: they might be mad at me, they might leave me, they might not like me. What then? I simply would tell myself, "Things were good, so why rock the boat?"

But were things really good?

When you neglect to acknowledge the reality of your outer world, your inner world is left to carry the negative energy of it, and is left in a continual feeling of unease.

I am now able to clearly see how I created my part in the past. I was very good at letting people push my buttons and limits, as I took most things to heart and allowed most things to land on me. I was not always able to speak up initially, especially if it was with people who were close to me. Ironically, I could speak up on the behalf of others if they were being mistreated somehow. Yet, I found it more difficult to do for myself. This silence would of course open the door for it to reoccur in the future, and by the second or third time I would be triggered faster and more strongly, which left me at times freaking out over something that seemed small to others, yet was now huge to me. As a result, at times I became someone I didn't want to be in the moment, as I could be led by the ego, which I would then feel guilty for after.

As time evolved and my inner awareness grew, I began to understand that this process was an unconscious and familiar pattern in me. In trying to keep the peace and everything happy, I was neglecting myself and my own feelings, which in turn created havoc within me. Fearing the outcome of speaking up was then emphasized in my mind by the stories I told myself, which then overrode and silenced my voice. My thoughts were that I would drive a wedge between myself and the people I loved by setting boundaries and that it would be much easier to just ignore my own feelings and move on. But was it really easier? What was I allowing by my silence? And what was I creating for myself? These thoughts created the dilemma I would feel within myself. How could I feel connected and loved and yet be seen for who I am? And what was I really afraid of by setting healthy boundaries?

It's ironic, because I found that what I really feared most was feeling unloved and disconnected, and I was totally unaware that I was creating that very thing for myself by not saying how I feel or setting boundaries.

The truth is that implementing healthy boundaries connects us, strengthens our relationships and allows us to be seen and accepted for who we are. They help to create relationships based on respect and understanding for all involved.

Where are you in setting boundaries?

Here is a simple exercise to try. Grab a pen and paper and follow these steps. Write down your answers to the following questions.

- How do I want to be treated by others?

- How am I actually being treated by others? (Be honest.)

Compare your answers. Then ask yourself:

- When, how and why have I allowed my boundaries to be crossed by others?

- What have I allowed even though I felt upset and what is stopping me from speaking my true feelings? Is there an inner fear I carry? If so, what is it?

Go deeper and connect to your true feelings. What are you afraid of? Did you know or feel in your gut that something was off when a line had been crossed but didn't say anything?

Be gentle with yourself as emotions and feelings arise. Try to keep the focus on you, and do not allow your mind to wander off with all the reasons why you couldn't set boundaries at the time (by blaming others). Focus on you and allow yourself to be really honest with yourself. Is a change or shift necessary? What can you do now to create the change? Show compassion to yourself and remind yourself that it's OK. You were not aware before, but now you are.

Choosing to shift how we navigate ourselves by setting boundaries may bring up guilt or shame at first. You may think, how can I do that? Fear may rise up in you; it's there to show you what may need looking at and what may lie beneath your inaction or inability to set healthy boundaries. Allow whatever energies you feel to move through you, acknowledge them and at the same time confirm to yourself why the boundaries are needed now.

Sometimes when we give too much, people please or believe that others are more important and deserving than us, we unconsciously allow ourselves to be mistreated or not seen. We can then feel guilty when we realize that what is happening is not OK or healthy, and we may want to change it. Remember, it's OK to say no and to ask for what you want or need. It's also OK to tell others what you feel is acceptable or unacceptable behaviour. Doing so is self-love, and when you are coming from a place of authenticity it is spoken with truth and kindness for all involved. There is no ego attached or angst or ugliness exhibited, and it therefore is more likely to be received as such by others.

It takes time to learn how to show others how we want to be treated, but it's important to do. So:

- Practice and allow yourself to communicate your needs clearly. It can help to work on clearing your third, fourth and fifth chakras with meditation, as this clears any blockages you may be unaware you are carrying. Your energy will then flow more freely through you, and outwardly as a result.

- Practice saying no and expressing yourself with truth, compassion and love, and yet without justification.

- Allow your feelings to be valid and important because they are. You matter!

- Believe in you—your true self, not your old patterns and beliefs.

- Notice how you feel when you are with certain people. What do you allow and why? Then practice stepping back emotionally or physically from a situation or person if needed. This can at times be the best way to allow healing within and to begin setting boundaries. Yes it may hurt, but it gives everyone involved the gift of time: time to be still, to quiet your mind and to open your heart; time to gain clarity and choose the best way to move forward, or not. Accepting what is and accepting where others are releases you from the anxiety of trying to change things. Trust that maybe being separate for the time being is what's really best, and know that it doesn't have to mean it's forever.

Always remember these two key traits that are needed to create healthy and better boundaries:

In order to be seen… you must SHOW who you really are.
In order to be heard… you must SPEAK authentically.

The Love Connection

As I moved through my self-love journey, I found the more I learned to love myself, the more my heart opened and I felt the connection we all share. The truth is, we are all one and we are all here to evolve into our truest version of ourselves. Connection with others, I believe, is also a part of healing and self-love. Because when you feel the love within yourself, you can also feel the deeper connection from others, and you can share it, thus expanding your heart. I recently watched a TV show where Adele was being interviewed. As I watched the interview, I could feel Adele's vulnerability and authenticity as she spoke. She too was on the other side of a painful life event and came out changed. I somehow felt drawn to her and felt like we were kindred spirits. Although she will probably never know me or about my journey, her story enriched my life with the connection we all have. It doesn't matter what your lifestyle is or the money you have or lack of it, we are the same and feel the same at our core.

I think it's amazing that people we regard as famous are speaking out and showing the real, more authentic sides of themselves. We are a world that somehow has been trained to believe that they are better than us and that they live a fairy tale life, which has always felt wrong or bizarre to me—even more so now. It's all in perception. The truth is, we all bleed when we are cut, whether this occurs on the outside or the inside of ourselves, and we then are left to tend to the healing of the remnants, scars or pain that is revealed. The more we love ourselves, the more we will open our minds and our hearts to see others and love them for who they are, not their labels or roles because we will know in our hearts that at our core, we are the same.

Gifts From Self-Love

- I have learned how to and am now able to give myself what I need, want and desire. I can easily give myself a hug when I feel I need one, and although it may sound silly to some, it actually helps. As it is the energy of the love behind a hug that heals, and if you are truly expressing this love to yourself, you can feel it. I now also buy myself flowers—just another loving gesture that I can give myself, and one that I would not have considered doing in the past. Most importantly, I give myself the gift of time: time to rest, time for play, time to love and be loved and time for connection with others, with nature and with myself. Taking the time to feel, listen and give myself what my body, mind, heart and soul need is self-love. Remember, when you don't give yourself what you desire, you are silently telling yourself that you are not worthy of it. Surrounding yourself with beauty and love creates the energy you live in, which you can then feel. I now take the time to embrace it all around me and focus consciously on it daily, whether that be through enjoying nature and feeling the warmth of the sun or spending time with my kids, grand kids, friends or family. It is all love. Simply receiving or reciprocating a smile from a stranger can bring a smile within. You never really know who's on the receiving end of the smile, and it is quite possible that you are unknowingly helping someone just by showing kindness.

- I have learned to be with myself and that being alone doesn't mean you are lonely. This took time as a lot of tears were released in the beginning. This is also not to say that I never feel lonely now—I can, but I also know the truth is that we are never alone if we include ourselves as someone, enjoy our own company, and feel connected to the universe. I have always loved connecting with people, meeting new friends and going to gatherings and still do, however, I have now also come to love quiet and stillness and I enjoy what it adds to my life. I like who I see in the mirror now, and I am able to reassure myself that I am always doing the best I can. When I feel off balance, I remind myself that I am proud of how far I've come and of my growth. By seeing myself with love and compassion I am able to receive love from others more freely and with a sense of warmth and gratitude, knowing I am worthy of it.

- I have learned to become more confident, independent and trusting in myself and my journey. I can see that I was exactly where I was meant to be during my time as a stay-at-home mom. Loving my children has been the biggest gift for me, and at times, they are where some of my biggest lessons and growth derive from. I now know and understand that I have always given love fully and easily—it's a part of who I am and who I continue to be. Learning to give that love from a place of authenticity rather than a place of fear or self-judgment has freed me from the shackles of mental self-sabotage and thinking that I need to be more. Seeing this pattern I carried allowed me to discover that at times my attempts to "be more or better" only distanced myself from the situation, others and myself.

- I have learned what I want in life and how to ask for it. This has been incredibly life changing for me. When you come from a genuine loving place, it is felt by others and even though you may be setting a boundary, it is usually accepted more easily. Honestly, it surprised me to learn how some of my old ways of thinking were skewed, a little backwards and mostly fear-based. Perception is everything, and a slight shift in how you see something can change everything for the better.

Throughout the years, I've frequently made lists of what I want to be, to do and to have in my life. I always find the lists interesting, even enlightening at times, as the lists are ever-changing. Yet, what seemed to stay the same was the longing I had for more joy, happiness and contentment. One particular day a couple of years ago, I was making my "to have" list and found that there was not a lot I could think of. The list was only one or two items, which felt odd to me. Then it hit me: I have everything I need! I really wanted for nothing. In that moment, a warm sensation rushed over me, and my body filled with a sense of peace and calm. It was an amazing awareness to behold. I realized that day that: *When you love what you have… you have everything you need!*

An amazing blessing to behold!

What do you want to create in your life? To be, to do and to have? Remember that your thoughts and words are energy, and when set with intention, they have the potential to become your reality.

Chapter 10
The "F" Word

Forgiveness *is*:

- FOR YOU, not them

- Knowing that your future happiness is more important than holding onto something that you cannot change.

- Key to healing the pain, moving forward and finding peace within.

Forgiveness *is not*:

- Saying that whatever happened was OK or right.

- Holding on to things or past events and wishing they could have been different than they were.

Where to Begin ...

I called this chapter "The 'F' Word" because forgiveness was a word I could not even say before embarking on my healing journey. When I would think about it, my body would contract and tighten, my stomach would feel nauseous and my mind would swirl with all the reasons why I shouldn't do it. I would be lying if I said it came easy to me. I have learned that forgiveness is very much a personal process and one that only you can decide how to do and when you are ready for it. For me, the more I looked inward and became aware of who I was and why I was that way, the more I realized that there were a few key people in my life that I needed to forgive in order to move forward.

For some of these people, I had no prior knowledge that I held anger for them inside. It was only after digging deep that I came to understand where some of my feelings and hidden wounds came from. This truth is not always easy to see or accept at first glance. Remember that we all form our own opinions or perceptions of people, events and ourselves, and when we see these in another light, it can be disillusioning at first. The stories we told ourselves and believed in years past may be ingrained in us, and we may hold onto them for various reasons. They may have justified our own actions, how we saw ourselves or how we wanted to see others. They may have helped us feel safe. There could be many layers to why we held onto old beliefs. I found that the more I was willing to open up these layers, the more that came up for me to look at, which felt overwhelming, disheartening and messy at times. Seeing with clarity allowed the real truth to emerge, which then allowed the story or illusion to begin to fade. What I found was that it also allowed me to see the bigger picture of how my thoughts intertwined to affect it all.

There are some who think that forgiveness makes you look weak, that the other person is "getting away" with something or "winning" by being forgiven. I know of people who have internalized and held onto all the hurt, pain or even trauma from things that happened many years ago. They've refused to look at anything except how they were wronged and to this day will still feel triggered when the subject arises. So, are they winning? Holding onto something for an extended period of time, long after it has occurred, is no longer about the actual deed of mistreatment or perceived betrayal. For it is in the past, and they have chosen, albeit unconsciously, to carry all the emotional baggage from it with them into their now.

There are limitless reasons that we believe why or how someone wrongs us, and because we are all unique beings with our own beliefs, we are all affected in different ways by each scenario. Although "betrayal" is a word that most people don't like to hear or ever want to be on the receiving end of, it is the word that is most used when we feel mistreated by someone. It can show up in many forms in our everyday lives, through friendships, work, spouses, family members and even betraying ourselves. Whether we are lied to, manipulated, cheated on, or feel like we were taken advantage of, it can be difficult at first to see or admit to ourselves that we've been betrayed. As we've previously discussed, we often only see the good in others, believing that they would never do anything underhanded or deliberately try to cause us pain. We can put blinders on, only seeing what we want to see, living in a bubble of sorts, all of which does not allow us to see the truth of our reality. We see only an illusion, and we create our part of it by unconsciously allowing it to continue.

The truth is that no one is perfect, nor can anyone live up to what you tell yourself or how you believe they are. However, when betrayal comes from someone you trust or love, it can feel initially like a sword has been plummeted into your heart, and it may feel like too much to handle. Your hurt heart can quickly be masked with anger. This is a form of self-protection, for it is easier to feel rage and blame someone than to allow yourself to feel vulnerable and deal with the true raw emotions you embody. It may be too painful to look at, and if it is, that's OK. Give yourself the gift of time and know that you are doing the best you can. Just be willing to check in again when you feel like you might be ready.

Self-betrayal is not something I really thought about in the past. However, I now believe it is something that we all do and experience from ourselves during our lives. By not allowing yourself to be who you are and by not giving yourself permission to be seen, heard and loved, you are indeed hurting yourself. You are unconsciously making yourself small because you believe you are small, and this is self-betrayal. Another aspect of self-betrayal can be seen outwardly. When our actions are based solely on our goals and objectives and not on how we feel, we are deceiving ourselves by thinking that the outside world is more important than our inner world.

Forgiving yourself, I've found, is essential in self-love. As you begin to realize the many times where you were not really yourself, or you felt unworthy, or you became invisible, or you perhaps allowed others to mistreat you, it can feel disheartening at first. It can bring up a sense of uneasiness, sadness or maybe anger at first, and it can make it difficult to see and accept who you were and what you allowed into your life. Yet, it is this awareness that is the doorway that leads you to discover who you truly are. It's imperative to be gentle with yourself, and if possible, see yourself through the eyes of compassion and understanding. The blessing is that you now have the opportunity and are willing to forgive, shift and grow from this awareness.

How do you know when you are ready to forgive? Well, let me counter that question with these: Do you find you are often thinking, *I'm tired of feeling this way, angry, resentful, sad or hurt?* Are you continually reliving everything in your mind or venting over and over to friends and feeling exhausted as a result? These may be signs that you are ready to forgive. The next step is to ask yourself, "Am I willing to *think* about forgiving?" How do you feel about asking this?

If you find that these questions bring up all sorts of emotions or feelings that are still too raw, that's OK! One day at a time. Again, this is a personal process with no set time limit or right or wrong way. You are doing it for you, so allow yourself to be who you are in each moment as you go through the process. Allowing yourself to be who you are is also a step, in that you are taking the time to notice and then release any stuck energy or resistance you are feeling that is in the way of you beginning the process of forgiveness. Remember there are many layers to healing.

So yes, before you can begin to forgive, it's important to give yourself time to grieve and release all the negative energy associated with the perceived wrong bestowed on you. Give yourself permission to let it all go and be who you need to be in the moment. If you feel angry, allow yourself to be, or if you find yourself in a puddle of tears, allow that too. If it helps, write down how you feel in a journal, or scream to the heavens—just release it all. (It feels good, honestly.) I had a therapist who once told me that I could benefit from joining a boxing class or punching bags, which I laughed at, at the time. Being a small-framed, five-foot-three woman, I could not see myself doing that. Although, I did tell her that I had been doing my own version of that on my own at home by punching my bed or pillows. Her response was, "Good for you!" It's healthy to release the strong emotions you feel in a safe manner. At the time, I had no idea that it was good for me or really understood why it was so helpful to release it or the energy around it, so I found it interesting that I somehow innately knew it was good for me and what I needed in the moment.

Writing down how I was feeling also helped me to release a lot of my stress in a safe way. As you are writing it, you are also speaking it in your mind, all of which is energy. Honestly, when it comes to releasing your initial feelings, there is no right or wrong way. Simply allowing yourself to be as you are and giving yourself the gift of time to grieve is what is important.

Yet, saying that, if a long time has passed and you still find you are in the pain and negativity of your story, it's important to notice your thoughts. Continual angry or resentful thoughts might be keeping you stuck in the past and filling your body with negative energy, which then creates and manifests more of the same for yourself in the present.

This saying helped me immensely: **Grief is normal—suffering is a choice.** There is definite truth to those words when you are able to understand the difference. Yet, you may find it hard to distinguish the difference in the beginning, when your hurt or pain is fresh. You may not have had a choice in what happened to you or around you, but you *do* have a choice in how you respond to it and what you create for yourself in the future. When we continually ruminate over things, we can begin to feel and act like a victim. If you notice this feeling rising up in you, that's OK. It simply means that you have created a story in your mind, and you now believe that it is true and a part of you. But know that victim mentality is only real in your mind. Noticing it and choosing to place your focus consciously on something else or reaffirming the truth to yourself can help shift it.

As we move through the beginning stages of our hurt and pain, we may receive attention, love or understanding from others, which is an amazing blessing to have. It absolutely helps to feel loved, understood and validated. Although, there can also be a flip side that may keep you feeling stuck. Sometimes, if others stay on the "mad train" with you, you may begin to feel justified in your thoughts and remain stuck in the past, unable or unwilling to forgive and move on. This kind of "support" may also have the potential to keep adding fuel to the fire, reigniting the story again and again, keeping you in it. Again, being heard and validated by a friend is great and very much needed, however if it leads you to feel self-righteous, and you find you are not willing to look inwards at yourself because you are "right," then you may have landed in the ego and your story will continue to be one of blame, trapping you in it. Self-awareness is key. It's important to notice how you feel and what you need as you move along in this process, as things do change. You may have needed to vent at the beginning, but take note, how does venting make you feel now? It is imperative to make yourself the priority and keep checking in with yourself. So, remember to ask yourself occasionally: "What or who am I needing *now* to move forward?" And then give it to yourself.

It's ironic, actually, because we think we are hurting those that wronged us by keeping our stories alive. But are we really hurting them? And what are we doing to ourselves by keeping the stories alive? It's been said that holding onto feelings of animosity, pain or revenge is like you are drinking poison and expecting others to die. We can hold on so tightly, not because we want to, but because we fear that our pain will be forgotten if we let go. We believe that if we do let go, the perpetrator of the pain will get off and be free to live their lives without accountability. When the hard truth of the matter is that they are most likely already doing that.

As you can see, forgiveness really is a personal process. There may be many layers to move through before you actually decide you are ready to tackle it. So, keep checking in with yourself and asking, "Am I ready to forgive?" And notice how your body feels asking the question. The day will come when you will feel ready to take the first step, so keep in mind that there's no time limit or right or wrong way.

When You Feel Ready: Accept and Surrender

Remember, **ACCEPTING** what has happened *does not* mean it was OK that it happened! But, when you refuse to accept and you resist the truth of a person or your situation, you hold yourself captive and become powerless to it.

When we encounter a painful event in our lives, it may feel almost impossible to accept it. Yet, if it is so painful, why do we hang onto it? What are we really resisting by not accepting it? Why can't we let it go?

Staying connected to the pain attaches us to our story and keeps it alive. It stays with us, in us and becomes us. We may feel a sense of safety in it somehow. We allow the story to continue even when the truth may now be different and things have changed or even after we have taken definite steps towards moving forward in our daily lives.

The story may still be there, thought about or verbalized to others when brought up in conversation. Why is it still there? Is there perhaps a deeper meaning to it? Sometimes it may simply be that you are not ready for the next stage of healing, and that's OK! Accept where you are and have patience, but also notice if it has become a new pattern of yours. Is the story you tell yourself your true reality now? Or is your mind keeping you in the past?

It may be helpful to ask yourself the following questions:

- Why am I struggling to let go and accept this? Is the story I'm tell myself defining me in some way? Giving me a stand? Or has a victim mentality become a new pattern?

- What am I holding on to by not letting go?

- Is there lingering hurt or pain that needs my attention? Or am I simply keeping past events alive to validate myself?

Try not to judge what you notice. Instead, be proud that you are taking steps and the time to raise your awareness!

SURRENDERING means accepting your life, yourself and what is. It allows your body and soul to feel at ease, as it is acknowledging that so much is out of your control.

Accepting and surrendering sound like easy things to do based on the given definitions, yet for me, they were two of the toughest aspects of my forgiveness process. I simply could not bring myself to accept the truth and what was happening in my life and unconsciously chose not to listen to how I was really feeling. I was resisting my life, and as a result, my mind and body remained in a constant state of stress. Continuous negative and low energy flowed throughout my body, and I didn't know how to change it. It seemed impossible to do at the time. I now know that I was letting go of my own power by resisting my reality and giving it away to others. I felt stuck and unhappy in the present because I was unable to accept and release the past.

When I was finally able to accept my reality, I could begin surrendering to it. I could let go of all the thoughts of why it should be different. I could see that so much was out of my control, and how I was giving my power away. This released some of the pressure and blame I had placed on myself, and in time I was able to then say, "OK, this has happened, it was hurtful, but what can I do now?" "What do I have control over?" When we open the door to options and give ourselves a choice, we begin to gain some of our inner power back. There is always a choice. We can stay in the pain, or we can choose to move forward. Changing the narrative of the story you tell yourself shifts how you see it. There is power in words!

For me, I became aware that I felt that if I let go of the story, then that was it—it would all be forgotten, and I would no longer be seen as someone wronged, which had become my definition of myself. It somehow felt better hanging onto it. I was still unable to see the underlying reason why I did this to myself. Which was if I let go of it, I would be left with myself, and that was my actual fear!! Hanging on to the story allowed me to stay in a place of safety and validation, where I did not have to take any steps into my new life, for my new reality is what I also feared. The irony is that my new reality was already happening, and I was actually already beginning to feel better, *just not yet in my mind.* The stuck energy of fear did not allow me to move into or see the present as it really was.

Surrendering is key to moving forward and creating the life we desire. The truth is that there is so much out of our control and so much we cannot change. Surrender to "what is" and allow your heart to once again be filled with the love that you are. We are all worthy of it, and we all have the power to do it!

What kind of future do you want or envision for yourself? It's for you to choose when you are ready. Celebrate your courage each step of the way and remember, don't "should" yourself. You are always exactly where you are meant to be and what you desire in your heart will become your reality when you are ready to let it in.

Opening Your Heart

These days, when I open the blinds of my living room window to breathe in the morning light, I gaze at the amazing scenery that I am blessed to wake up to every morning. The trees are full and lush with leaves dancing in the slight breeze. The morning sun shimmers on the water and illuminates the trees, bringing everything to life. It's so tranquil and beautiful!

It reminds me that it was not too long ago that I was unable to see the beauty that was in front of me. My heart and mind were closed, and you cannot see or feel with a closed heart and mind. It is the same premise with forgiveness. You cannot look at things with a closed heart and mind and expect them to ever change. Opening your mind to see the whole picture, forgiving yourself and finding compassion for yourself will then begin to open your heart.

Sometimes, when we have been hurt by someone, it can feel difficult to see past the pain. It can fog our vision. A story is set in your mind and does not waver. But compassion can clear the fog and allow clarity to emerge. When you are able to see yourself through the eyes of compassion, you can then begin to see others the same way and start to realize that perhaps they are not bad people, but rather that they simply made bad choices. Seeing people as they are and becoming aware of the unconscious nature they carry with them does not change the fact that they may have wronged or deceived you, but it does allow you to understand and see them more clearly.

What does change is how you view and continue to experience the story. When you are aligned with your true self and are able to stand in your own power, you are simply no longer triggered by the past. When your heart is open, you may even begin to notice a slight feeling of sadness for others, knowing that they too could change and grow if they so choose. Finding compassion for others, like forgiveness, is for you. It doesn't mean that anything in your outside world has to change, that you have to be best friends with those who have wronged you, or even have them in your life. Compassion is a personal gain that releases you from the bondage of the pain and lightens your heart, mind, body and spirit. It allows you to move forward without resentment and with knowing in your heart that: *Hurting people hurt people.*

Letting It All Go

When you are able to accept, surrender and find compassion and love for yourself, the road to forgiveness becomes easier to navigate. When you see others as you see yourself, your heart begins to soften.

Occasionally, we must forgive without receiving an apology, which is *tough*. In this situation, it is important to be honest with yourself about the truth of the situation, the other person or people and yourself—what really happened? Past that, know that the more you love yourself and remind yourself that you are worthy, with or without an apology, the easier you will see that maybe the other party is simply not capable of giving you an apology. Remember, everyone can only give from where they are and from the level of conscious awareness that they have at the time. Remember also that what someone does to you has nothing to do with you—it has to do with their own character and unconscious nature.

There is no recipe to follow when you are wanting to forgive someone or yourself. Just be willing to listen to yourself, your body and your soul. Believe me, I was all over the place, so I simply followed what I felt I needed as each day passed. Some days it was stillness; others it was meditation or healing music. One practice I found very helpful was writing a letter to the person I felt had wronged me or to myself (or both). I would express all of my emotions freely, without thinking or editing, just writing. Then I would read the letter out loud and allow whatever emotions I was feeling to come up and flow through myself. No holding back. Sometimes I would read it again. Then I would rip the letter up or burn it, releasing the pain and energy contained within it. This, I found to be very healing. I did it several times in the past, as I found it really helped to release my stuck negative and low energy. If you decide to try this too, it's important to just let your pen do the writing, and allow whatever comes out to be as it is. Don't think or edit it, just let your emotions and energy flow through you and release it.

There are many helpful tools to help guide you as you navigate forgiveness: Meditations, books and videos, for example. The important thing is not really what you do, but to listen to how you feel, love yourself along the way and give yourself the gift of time to figure it all out.

I'd like to leave you with one thought: There are always blessings in the pain! Yes, they may be near impossible to see if you're now facing a challenging or painful event, (believe me, I know) and maybe they still will be hard to see for a long time after it, and that's OK. Trust me though, they are there and in time you will see them.

So love yourself always, and allow yourself the time to heal, forgive and open your heart to allow compassion in, both for yourself and others. You are worth it!

Forgiveness sets you free to live.

Chapter 11

Sensing, Seeing and Connecting

INTUITION

The ability to know something without having proof. It is to know something or to consider something likely from an instinctive feeling rather than from conscious reasoning. I look at intuition like a muscle: the more you allow yourself to feel and use it, the stronger it becomes. Hearing, listening and following intuition becomes more natural as you begin to trust it and yourself. Choices become easier and life is able to flow with ease.

The truth is, we all are intuitive, and we all make the choice whether to listen to our intuition or not. Regardless of our choice, it is something that is always there. It is the silent voice or feeling that arises within and brings awareness to us about a situation, a person or ourselves. It may be present in the moments when you find yourself saying, "I'm not sure why I did that, but I just knew somehow that I should," or perhaps when you've had a bad feeling about a person and you choose not to associate with them, only to find out later that it was a good choice. At times, it can be referred to as a gut feeling or a sense. This is intuition, a deeper knowing at the level of the soul.

We all have random thoughts and ideas that float through our minds, but sometimes we may feel particularly drawn to certain ones. Intuition leads us, and it may stir up some feelings of uncertainty or fear if the ego gets involved. Yet, if we continue and come to understand the fear, why it's there and become present, we will then be able to feel what our intuition would actually like to become known to us or within us. It's important to allow space for that to happen. You will somehow know that whatever your intuition is nudging you towards will be good for you, even without really knowing why or what the outcome will be.

I have always felt intuition strongly throughout my life, although like many, I didn't always listen to it. But I now realize that learning to listen to it, and strengthening it, is part of our journeys also. Our paths are not straight, nor are they always clear. Instead, they may feel difficult to understand. They may consist of many turns and do-overs. So, be willing, if you can, to allow yourself to embrace each of them. What you long for is on the other side.

A perfect example of this for me is birthing this book. I wholeheartedly believe that I have been led to this point in my life where I am now writing to help others. Looking back, I am able to see that I have had an ongoing abundance of help and guidance from various sources to get me to where I am today. I am also able to recognize that I just *knew* and felt that what I was doing and the choices I was making would be right for me, even though they didn't come with a clear road map.

Between Intuition and Fear

How can we distinguish between intuition and thoughts that come from the ego (fear)? Deciphering which thought or feeling is your intuition or if it comes from the ego and is fear based can seem difficult, but they are actually felt very differently within. Thoughts that come from the ego are always lacking and embody low energy such as anger, worry, self-absorption or self-righteousness. They may make you feel like you *need* to make a decision or do something. Intuition is a knowing. It is a feeling that you should or shouldn't move towards something and is felt more gently within. It is a gut feeling that nudges you forward or away from potential danger, or it can be a feeling that you have that something feels off somehow. You may feel some fear around this deeper knowing though, as the mind (ego) will sometimes come up with reasons against it or why you should or shouldn't do something. When this happens, simply become curious and ask yourself questions about these reasons. Where do they come from? Are they valid, or are they just things you want or need to believe to feel safe? How do these thoughts make you feel?

There may be times when you choose not to believe the truth of your intuitive feelings and instead push them away. Perhaps a friend or loved one's true actions or intentions are being hidden, but you can feel that something is off. Your mind (ego) will tell you, "No, no, it's OK; everything is fine," but your intuition will be nudging you to investigate. You may intuitively know the truth, but choose not to see or believe it. In recent years I have learned to follow my intuition, and although it sometimes uncovered things that I did not want to see or know at the time, I am now thankful for the truth, and the growth and lessons it has taught me.

We are a society that is collectively growing, learning and evolving. We are all longing for peace and contentment in our lives, to have it all and to somehow do everything perfectly. The reality is, that this is unattainable if you live from your ego. Why? Because there is never enough when fear is the driving force behind your decisions. Alternatively, your intuition will always feel right. You may not know why, but you can absolutely feel it. When you follow it, everything works out with ease and feels better for everyone involved. That's not to say it always works out how you "thought" it should, or want it to, but it leads you on a truer, more authentic path.

Be Still and Listen

Our guardian angels and spirit guides have miraculous ways to connect and converse with us, and when we are open in our hearts and ready and willing to receive them, they will do so. I have heard others talk of a subtle, clear voice that they have heard from outside themselves at times. This voice sounds real, as if there is someone there talking to them; a gentle, calm voice that guides them on paths. I have heard this voice myself, both from within, and also a voice from the outside of myself in the past years, and as a result, I have come to trust it.

The first time I heard it, it moved me to listen to my intuition and seek the truth at a time when I felt terrified to have the truth revealed to me. I heard the words, "Yes, do it," spoken to me. The words felt so real to me. At that time, I had no idea how or why I was hearing these words, yet the calmness and softness in which they were spoken helped me to feel that everything would be OK somehow. Seeing the truth is not always easy, and may feel painful as it brings awareness to us that we perhaps are not wanting to see. Yet, for me at this time, it also revealed the doorway out of the bubble of illusions I had created for myself.

The second time I heard the voice, I believe it was testing me to see if I was listening. I was leaving my lake and I was exiting the park, when I heard a voice simply say, "Makeup." I remember vividly thinking, *What?* I paused for a moment because this voice felt like a true person speaking to me. I thought, *I packed my makeup, didn't I?* I decided to turn my car around and head back to the trailer just in case, and lo and behold, my makeup was still in the bathroom cabinet.

The third time was when I was leaving a friend's place after visiting. As I got into my car, I heard the words, "check your phone." I was in a hurry, so I didn't listen and drove off. Later on, when I went to use my phone, I could not find it. As you can imagine, I began to panic. I started going over all the places where I could have possibly left it or lost it, and then I recalled hearing the voice asking me to check it as I left my friend's. I soon discovered that I had indeed left it there. Now, the moral of the story is not that I found my phone, although that was a good outcome. No, the moral is that if I had truly listened to the voice, then I would have taken the moment to check for my phone, notice that it was missing and saved myself the time from having to drive back to her place to pick it up. Lesson learned and trust gained!

There is yet another way, I've found, that our spirit or soul can move through us. This "feeling" may be felt when our energies are aligned, and we allow it to flow through us. This is something that I experience frequently now, and I try to allow it to flow through me freely, when possible. I first became aware of this urge or feeling as I began to connect more within. I became more aware that I can feel the energy of my words and felt urges to reveal them and share them with others. This "feeling" could be felt quite strongly at times, and even though my ego did rise in the beginning and tell me, "No, no, Bevy, they don't want to hear this," I still felt that sharing was the right thing to do. Most often, I would share through text messages, and the words would come so easily and truthfully that it could surprise me, in that, at times I didn't think they sounded like me. I found I would often explain myself to others by saying, "I'm not sure where this is coming from, but I just felt like you needed to hear it." It felt like it came from another side of me—and really.... how true that is! I now understand that those words come from my soul or my higher self. They move through me and are meant to be heard by others. Sharing these words, I believe was the beginning nudge that I needed to believe in myself and to show me that I do have something worth sharing, as I was always met with gratitude for them. The truth is, I've always had the gift of gab, but I have now found the same in writing. What a gift!

The Signs Along the Way

As you allow yourself to listen to and trust your feelings, you may begin to notice a growing sense of awareness around you. You may be able to see and experience things differently. I would often be wondering how to do something or whether it was the right time for something when the universe would lovingly show me answers by way of signs. These signs would show up in the form of people, books, spoken words or actual signs, such as seeing a phrase, a reminder or written words of wisdom somewhere. There were also times when the signs were not so tangible or visible to the naked eye, but were instead the inability to move towards what I thought I wanted. Being met with a shut door does only make you push on it harder, as you think it should open. It can be a more difficult sign to recognize, or at least it was for me, because when we feel driven to something that does not truly serve us and is therefore not given to us, we seem to want it more, and we can feel very let down when we cannot have it. Yet, the simple truth is, even though that door is not meant for us, there may very well be a better door to go through in the future.

I remember when buying our first home, I thought the first house we saw was the one for us. I was heartbroken when we didn't get it. Yet, the next house we found was actually the absolute perfect fit for us and our family. I soon forgot about the other one. In fact, I was happy that the first deal had fallen through, otherwise we wouldn't have found the second one. I've always believed that everything happens for a reason, but now I can better understand why.

Signs are not necessarily directly in your face or do not explain to you exactly what steps to take next. Although they do sometimes appear or occur that way too. I've found that they are more often subtle hints or intuitive hits. The thing is when you ask the universe a question or for a sign, you then have to be open and aware to see it when it is delivered. As I've mentioned, signs can show up in various forms, from sudden epiphanies to things you read, hear or see. And if you miss a sign, don't worry, the universe will supply you with more, as it is always, ever gently nudging you forward. Remember, free will is always yours, and there is no one right path or decision. You always have the power to choose, and choose again.

The below phrase was sent to me from a friend among the chaos of the unfolding of my marriage. She sent it in a text, and it was a picture of a sign with these words written on it in chalk. Although I strongly felt it was a sign of future things to come, I was not in a place to act on it or truly understand it in the moment.

> *One day you will tell your story of how you've overcome what you are going through now, and it will become part of someone else's survival guide.*

Fast forward to now, and as the thought of writing a book came to my mind periodically, I would think, *Can I do it?* I found myself struggling with the thought of it, as I could also feel fear rise in me with every thought or possibility, yet it felt possible at the same time. One day, as I was pondering the possibility a little more seriously, I received two text messages simultaneously. One was from a friend, thanking me for a text I had previously sent her and expressing how she felt that my words had truly helped her. The other was from my daughter, answering me with what she thought about me writing a book. She wrote, "Yes, Mama, do it! You have lots to say. I'd buy it!" The timing of both texts was impeccable and literally brought me to tears. My first thought was, *OK, thank you. This is a sign, right?* Although this experience made me feel more intrigued about the idea of writing a book, I was still unsure about my ability to actually accomplish it all. This was not something in my comfort zone—it was unlike anything I'd ever done or contemplated doing before. So, I continued to sit with my thoughts and also with the fear that I found accompanied every thought I had.

Days later, I received an email from Lee Harris, an amazing energy intuitive that I had just finished a course with, that asked the question in the title, "Are you serious about writing a book?" When I opened it, I saw that he had included information about a course on writing your own book. *What?* I thought. In the coming days, I kept gravitating back to the email, yet I was still not feeling secure or confident in the idea. Then, a few days later, I was led to look back at the above words my friend had said to me. It had now been a few years since they had been sent to me, yet as I read them again, I felt the connection to them, and I absolutely knew without a doubt that it was meant to be. Writing a book was the next step on my path.

The many signs I've received along my path has been incredible, and I would like to share one more with you that still leaves me in awe today when I think about it.

It was when I began to think about renovating the outside of the mobile home—maybe paint, add a new deck, landscape? I knew it needed it, and I wanted to do it, yet, I had found myself having second thoughts continually. *Should I? It will cost too much!* I had a vision, but my mind would not let me begin to create it. It was a constant back and forth in my mind. *OK, I'll do it,* then, *Hmm, maybe not.* I was very aware of how it brought up fear in me, as it was my first big renovation by myself. The old patterns I carried within me were there once again, which were uncomfortable to face, yet I also knew that they were there to simply show me that there is more to heal. I could feel myself contracting within my body as my mind was telling me all the reasons why I shouldn't do it. There was the devil and the angel again (ego and my soul), or at least that's how I explained it to myself back then. Then one day I was driving back from a beautiful weekend at the lake, where I was full of thoughts around the subject. *Should I?* was my last thought, when I finally said to myself, "Just leave it, Bevy. You'll know when it's the right time."

Well, I kid you not, as I drove into the city, I came up to a stop sign, and there was a car stopped in front of me. As I pulled up behind him, I glanced down at his licence plate, and it read: "It's Time". Honestly, I can't make this up. It still sends chills through me as I'm writing these words. I remember sitting there for a moment, in awe and giggled. Without hesitation I said out loud to myself, "OK, I'll do it," looked up and said, "Thank you!"

I found the perfect person to do my renovations. He was so efficient and easy to work with, and felt I could trust him. That was very important to me. He did beautiful work!

The trailer has made its transition from ours to mine, and I love it more than ever. The past memories remain a beautiful part of it, yet I am very much present and embracing where I am now and the new memories to come.

Keeping the trailer has taught me to trust myself, to rebloom the confidence that I had lost and become independent and loving to myself. It solidified my trust in myself, the universe and strengthened my intuition and inner knowing.

If you believe it… you too will see it!

Know and have faith that the signs you see along your path are for you. They may not always be seen the same way by others, and that's OK. If you know in your heart that something is a sign meant for you, then it is. When you surrender to and trust in the universe and yourself, miracles can happen, and there is no limit to what you can achieve.

Our Connected Journeys

The pandemic and how we each uniquely experienced it in our everyday lives may have differed completely. Yet at times, how we all felt within ourselves, both emotionally and physically with each experience was very much the same. Prior to it, we were all living life, working, enjoying family and friends, and perhaps travelling. Then, one day without warning everything changed. In a blink of an eye, life as we knew it stopped. Shock, fear, grief, anger and confusion were seen and felt everywhere, and in everyone, including myself. It was a pivotal time for me as I had been shifting and healing for a couple years, and I had gained self-awareness when the pandemic was at the beginning stages. So, I found that at times it was like I was watching it all unfold through two separate views: conscious and unconscious.

As we moved through the days and months, I could feel that the world's collective energy was based in and consumed by fear. Fear of it all: potential sickness, changes to daily life, the possibility of losing loved ones and moving on without them. Fear of the future, as it felt unknown and scary.

I remember feeling particularly sad and a bit stuck in negative, low energy one day after having had conversations with friends and family about how they were feeling and experiencing everything going on. As I sat on my couch afterwards thinking about them, I became overwhelmed with emotions, and it was at that moment that the thread that ties us all together was revealed to me. I became aware that the greater portion of the collective was feeling a lot of the same emotions and feelings that I too had experienced a few years prior, when my marriage ended. True, they are not at all the same events on the outside. Yet, the negative, low energies of shock, fear, confusion and sadness that were embodied by most as a result of the pandemic were very much the same as what I experienced inside with ending of my marriage. I was able to understand how others felt, as I had been them previously. Unconsciously, I had been navigating my life in the same emotional shoes, feeling stuck and fearful, not too long ago. It too had been my experience that one day I was living and enjoying my life, and then seemingly out of nowhere, that ended. When life as we know it changes, with or without warning or for any reason, we are faced with rebalancing and regaining our sense of being grounded in who we are and where we are headed.

This new awareness shifted me, in the sense that I could see and feel our connection. I could see how fear was prevalent and ruminating was continual in many people, and I absolutely felt it too—there was a lot to deal with. Yet, I could also see that this was another sign that my painful experience had happened for a reason.

The pandemic opened up the wounds of the collective (everyone) and was extremely difficult to navigate and move through at the time. And yet, the thoughts, actions, reactions and emotions we had during it, or perhaps still have, are now opportunities to get to know ourselves and bring awareness to us. If you still feel fear or are stuck somehow, I encourage you to search within yourself for answers. Ask yourself the following questions and then notice what feelings or energies arise, and allow them to do so.

- How did I react or not react?

- What was my experience?

- How did I perceive and move through it all?

- What did certain events bring up in me?

- Was I consumed with fear, anger or maybe denial? Am I still?

- Am I carrying the wounds of it all into my now?

I remember having a conversation with my daughter, who was at the time, feeling overwhelmed and stressed working in healthcare, as many in that industry were. I reminded her, "What we are facing now will pass and come to an end, and who you will be then will be determined by who you are now." You can choose the fear and allow it to embody and become a part of you, or you can see it when it arises, feel it and be willing to also help yourself find calm in the chaos. Find a moment to be still, breathe and remind yourself, "Yes, this is happening, but I am OK!"

Remember, when something happens around us, it may not directly affect us in this moment, yet it may feel like it does. That feeling comes from the energy we embody from everything and everyone around us and from our own thoughts, words and stories we tell ourselves about what's happening. Fear then rises and the mind comes up with the best way to continue forward, usually by choosing between avoiding, fighting or fleeing. This fear may lead you to judge others, and equally, we too may be judged for our decisions. This unfortunately can lead to separation, for when this begins both sides are in the grips of the ego and cannot see their way out.

Can you be willing and allow yourself to see the reflection in the mirror? In other words, can you see that what they are mirroring back to you is indeed you? True, you may be on the other side of the fence with your opinion, yet both defensive actions and reactions are equally governed by the ego, otherwise division would not exist. Could you consider what would happen if you instead were able to accept who or where the other party was in the moment? How would this change how you feel? How would you then respond? You would not necessarily be agreeing with them, but rather you would be able to hear them and yet stand in the power of you, by not allowing their thoughts and perceptions to land on you. How would this change the dynamics of your discussion?

I invite you to shift your perception slightly. Be willing to see through a different lens, expand your mind ever so slightly to the good side of the so-called bad. If you are unable to, that's OK. Simply begin to investigate the resistance or fear that's attached around those thoughts.

Here are a few things I gained by shifting my perception around the pandemic:

- **Solitude.** It was extremely difficult at times, as it was not by choice. Although, in time I was able to learn to sit with the stillness and silence and found, there were moments when I was able to feel OK within it. It taught me that being alone does not have to mean you're lonely. I instead chose to take the time to expand my growth, both personally and spiritually, something I'm not sure I would have done had the world kept spinning as normal.

- **Slowing down.** Yes, we were forced into it, and yes, it may have felt like a bad thing initially. But can you expand your view to notice what we gained? There was more family time and less stress from not running around to keep up with the business of life and schedules of the kids. The things that we deemed important and thought we needed to do, be or have in our lives before were suddenly put on hold, and the void that was left behind was an opportunity to embrace more ease and time for inner reflection. It gave us a chance to look at what is "really" important to us. For me, this allowed me to look at and ask myself, what do I *really* want in my life? What is important to me and for my family, and am I creating it? If not, what can I do or shift to make it a reality? I now feel the slowing down phase within the pandemic gave me the time needed to allow these thoughts to percolate in my mind, raise my energy and to then integrate that positive energy within my mind and body, thus allowing my desired reality to manifest in the future.

- **Well-being.** I began taking online courses to further myself personally, as well as my spiritual growth. I also liked doing online activities such as zumba, qigong, yoga and various exercises. The personal and spiritual courses helped me in another way, as I had the time to learn how to navigate what some might deem as the basics of technology. Patience and laughter were needed, and ultimately found. As a result, I no longer feel scared to try new things and have learned that you never really know what you like or what you are good at until you try it. Doors open when you face the uncomfortable feelings of the unknown.

We all experienced the pandemic years differently, and my heart truly goes out to anyone who has suffered or felt extreme loss as a result of them. We were all affected in ways that were personal to us. Some were unable to say goodbye to loved ones, and for so many reasons, that is unacceptable to me. At a time when we needed to feel connected, we were separated, and that is truly disheartening. If this was your experience, from my heart to yours, let me send you big hugs and remind you that love is energy—it has no boundaries. It expands through us and is felt in the hearts of the ones we care about and love, whether we are physically with them or not.

As we move forward together in gaining conscious awareness, we will need compassion and love for everyone, including ourselves. Where are you now? Has fear of the past been carried into your present? If so, how is it affecting you? I encourage you to seek any and all types of professional help, if needed; to choose something that you deem as valuable and will allow you to understand and heal these aspects of you. Healing your inner self, at times, may go much deeper than we know. So, love yourself always and give yourself what you need to heal, to grow and to flourish. When you do, it will have the potential to expand to others, as your energy will be one of higher vibration and felt by everyone you encounter.

Yes, the biggest gift we can give to others is to love ourselves! For when we choose to do so, we become a part of the change we wish to see and create for the future. Each life you touch today with a loving hand or heart will lead the way for others to follow and do the same.

Chapter 12
The Loving Hearts Along the Way

THE BIGGER PICTURE

The people we encounter in our lives are all there for a reason. Some we feel blessed to have met, and some we may wish we hadn't. And yet, it is often the ones we wish we could have avoided that teach us the most.

I believe the universe always gives us who or what we need at any given moment. When we need a helping hand, a hug or to learn something new, it will show up, yet not always as we expected. So, it's up to us to see it as such and embrace it. Free will is always ours.

There is an abundance of people who come into our lives, and each one is there for either a reason, a season, or a lifetime. Ultimately, we will grow in some way with each one. Whether it's a loving or difficult experience we share, the lessons we learn together will shape us a little more and help us to grow.

In the last few years I have been blessed with many people showing up in my life to help, guide or love me along the painful path I found myself on. During it, I was simply thankful when something worked out or if I had a friend to lean on. Now, I'm still thankful for all of that, but I am also thankful for the universe's hand in it, as it is ever so clear to me that there was indeed divine timing at play.

A Reason

There are countless people that I met along my healing path who showed up at just the right moment to say the words I needed to hear, or to simply share a smile or a hug through their eyes. These people had no idea who I was or why I was sobbing, angry or unable to find a solution for whatever I was attempting to accomplish. Yet, they exuded compassion and understanding towards me in the very moment I needed it. For a brief moment they were in my day, and that moment will forever be remembered with a warm heart. I'd love to tell you about all of them, however, I will limit myself to sharing two that shine brightly in my mind.

I was driving home one day from the doctor's during the chaos of my divorce, when all of sudden I became what I can only describe as hysterical, overwhelmed and shaky. It was a time when the reality of my life was becoming very real to me, and I felt incredibly alone and unloved. I came to a red light, and there was one car ahead of me. As I sat trying to calm myself and to get the flood of water from my eyes to stop so that I could see the road clearly, I saw a young woman in the car ahead of me open her car door and come towards me with a box of tissues in her hand. I rolled down my window and was met with a kind soul who also offered me her heart. She had no idea what had happened or why I was crying. She didn't know anything about me at all. And yet there she was, standing before me offering me a tissue and asking if she could call someone to pick me up or even give me a ride home herself. I was only blocks from my home, so I thanked her so much, but let her know I'd be OK. As she walked back to her car, I remember feeling in awe of what had just happened. At a time when I was being shown unloving, uncaring actions by others, the truth was revealed to remind me that I am worthy of love! The young woman, whom I will never know, was absolutely heaven-sent!

My other story takes place in the fall of my first year on my own. It was my first time taking my car in to change the summer tires to winter ones. Although this was not a hard task to do on a normal day, my days at the time were still anything but normal. I can see now that my thoughts that day were of anger and frustration about having to carry and lift the winter tires into my car—rubber on rubber does not move easily—and I was creating my day with that negative energy. However, I managed to get them into my car and the tires were changed successfully. When I came home, I opened my trunk to put the summer tires back into the shed and found them wedged together so tightly that I could not even begin to move them to get them out. I pushed, pulled and tried to grasp any part of them without success. There was no one around at the time; the streets were silent and bare. When I think about it now, I realize I could have knocked on a neighbour's door and asked for help, but again, my mind could not find easy solutions at the time as it didn't allow me the space for rational thinking. So, I continued yanking at the tires, becoming more and more frustrated with each attempt. To me, each time I tried solidified in my mind that I was alone. This allowed the fear, anger and frustration in my mind to rise to exorbitant proportions, leaving me feeling even more unhappy with myself and my inability to move the tires, and therefore angry with my life as it was. Tears flowed and my frustration turned to a feeling of inner rage with each passing moment that I stood there. I began hitting the tires, expecting somehow that they would jump out of the trunk by themselves.

During all of this, I was totally unaware that my neighbour had just pulled into his driveway. We hadn't met yet, but he walked right up to me and simply said, "Here, let me help you." Those words stayed with me. Not one question was asked, even though I'm sure he saw me beating up the tires as he drove up and the black mascara running down my face told the rest of the story. Words were not spoken, he simply moved the tires into the shed for me, and as he walked away he turned around and said, "If you ever need anything, just knock on my door." He was the hug I so desperately needed that day. I felt his heart without knowing it.

I believe that these two people were angels sent from heaven, because that is exactly how it felt in the moment. There are countless others that were absolutely there for me for various reasons and in the exact moments that I needed them. These angels swooped in and shared their kindness, compassion and hearts with me and I am thankful for each one.

When life gives you a chance, I encourage you to spread your wings and be an angel for someone else too. You never know the impact it will have.

A Season

There are also people who come into your life for a certain length of time before either leaving completely or their presence shifts or changes as time evolves. These people are also in your life for a reason and are instrumental in your evolution and growth. Their presence or their absence will undoubtedly either change you, how you see yourself or how you see your life moving forward.

When it was suggested to me by a dear friend to take a mindfulness meditation class, I had no idea what it entailed or what it would do for me. It was something I had never considered in the past and was not in my realm of thinking at the time. I simply said yes to the opportunity because I felt desperate to feel better. I had no idea that it would be the first step and doorway to the start of my healing.

I remember walking into the class for the first time, and somehow I knew I belonged there. I felt a loving, calm and easy energy in the room and coming from the instructor before me, Wonnita. I felt immediately drawn to her. As we went around the room introducing ourselves, I remember sitting there dreading having to talk about myself and share who I was or why I came to the class. When it came to my turn, my words came out in a brief jumble of emotion before I immediately started to cry. I felt embarrassed and somewhat ashamed for this, but as we continued on with introductions, I was shocked when two others also showed their vulnerability with tears. It became evident to me that although we were all different and had all joined the class for our own reasons, we were somehow connected.

With baby steps, Wonnita guided me to find a sense of ease, which was something I hadn't been able to acquire for myself up to that point. The door was opening slowly for me, and with much practice, determination and most importantly patience, I felt my inside begin to expand and my energy shift, which flourished into a craving for more. I spent the next couple of years continuing to learn with her, but I also began to expand my network of teachers. I began watching, reading, listening to lessons and meditating more with other spiritual teachers like: Eckhart Tolle, Wayne Dyer, Abraham Hicks, Louise Hay and Deepak Chopra and countless others, every day. They became a part of my daily routine as I spent many many hours learning, absorbing and integrating their wisdom, allowing it to become mine. These teachings became a very important aspect of my days and have transformed not only myself, but how I live my life. This transformation allowed me to gain more confidence, and I have since expanded my knowledge, growth and wisdom further through various on-line courses. I have discovered that you are never too old to learn and grow!

Yes, the people we meet on our path are always there to teach, love or help us grow somehow. Wonnita and I became close friends during this time, which to me was an added blessing. I truly believe our meeting was divinely guided and meant to be. We were put on each other's paths when the time was right. She was the key that opened the door and brought mindfulness, spirituality and stillness into my days when I needed it most, and she was an integral part to me starting the next cycle of my life.

Her presence in my life has shifted as the miles between us have grown, yet she is and will forever be in my heart and a part of my journey.

A Lifetime

As I sit here pen in hand, writing and connecting my thoughts to those who have been in my life for years, my heart is filled with warmth and love. I have been blessed with a lot of wonderful people throughout my life, some of whom I've grown up with since childhood. We made our way through adolescence, into adulthood, and have remained friends throughout marriages, kids and all of the other life events that happened along the way. We grew up together in a sense, and I now understand the deeper connection we share: our soul connection. We were meant to be in each other's lives to teach each other, love each other and help each other grow and evolve. For when we are with others for what feels like a lifetime, there are ebbs and flows to navigate within our relationships, and these are there to strengthen us.

Although this is true, there are also people that I've met later in life, and yet still feel this same strong bond and connection with. Within all of these people, I've found that when the chips are down and you are in darkness, there are a select few people that somehow shine through. They are the ones that are there by your side every step of the way. Understanding, giving guidance or expressing the things you really don't want to hear, but need to hear. They are the people who see you at your worst and somehow love you anyways—without judgment. I am blessed with a few such people. Whether I have found myself drowning in a puddle of tears, shouting angrily at the world or venting verbal diarrhea that I know sometimes made no sense to anyone but me, they have given me a loving ear. They have accepted me, along with every crazy text and phone call, allowing me to release the negative energy that was ravaging within me. I felt heard and loved always, even when there were no answers to be found.

The best way I can explain what I felt like was:

> They were simply and unconditionally in my car with me as I drove aimlessly with no clear direction or path. They lent me their ears, their hearts and their understanding as we drove together along the road that I call my journey.

I am eternally grateful for each of these special friends and the love they have added to my life, both then and now. We are meant to be together and I believe they are part of my soul family.

There is one more kind of relationship that we are blessed to have for a lifetime, and it is one that I now believe to be the most important relationship. That is, the one we share with ourselves. It truly is the most intimate relationship you will ever have. If you think about it, we share everything with ourselves. We love, we grow and we learn what sets our hearts on fire, and we gain wisdom to take us through the decades. Throughout the years, we will be our own best friend, and sometimes, our own worst friend. Through it all, we will begin to realize that some of our biggest lessons and opportunities for growth came from what we considered to be the most difficult times in our lives. For it is in those difficult times that we sometimes find the strength we didn't know we had. So, embrace today, be proud of who and where you are, open your heart and release what no longer serves you. Be your own best friend!

Chapter 13
The Energy of Joy

Finding Your Niche

We all have something we love to do that brings us a feeling of joy and contentment. The thing that we may at times feel we can get lost in, that can make us lose track of time or our surroundings doing. The thing that brings passion and aliveness into our days or ourselves. Have you ever wondered how our favourite activities do this for us? Well, as we've learned, everything is energy and this energy flows in and around us as we engage in different activities. The words, sounds and vibrations from these activities resonate with where we are or where we'd like to be. So, whether you are jogging, gardening, reading, meditating or doing whatever it is you love doing, if you are in the moment and aligned with the energy of it, it will flow through you, allowing joy in.

For me, I have always loved and enjoyed music. I find I can get lost in the moment when around it, as it's always been my happy place. It has been a part of my life ever since I was a little girl, whether I was listening to it or dancing along with it. Although, it was not until recent years that I became aware that music is actually more to me. Not only do I love it, but I can now feel my energy rise with the vibration emitted from the music and words. Listening and dancing to music has now become a form of healing and self-love that I give myself. It releases the negative energy in my body, clears my mind and raises my vibration, leaving me to feel amazing!

I've always been privileged to have music in my life and now I understand why: you attract what you are aligned with. I have fond memories from when I was young of guitar and fiddle playing at the farm where my dad grew up, which is where I first learned the two-step and polka and was amazed while watching others dance the jig. Although, it was during the pandemic that I finally made the true connection between dance and the healing it brings me. I decided to make a feel-good playlist for myself that I could listen and dance around my condo to when I found myself feeling low, fearful or scared. I found it could literally shift my energy within minutes. I would dance around my condo when I felt I needed a boost. Which quite honestly, is something I would not have been able to say out loud in the past as I gave others' opinions too much power over me. Now, I am proud that I do this for myself, as I believe it's an act of self-love.

It has been said many times that music soothes the soul. I have always believed that and now am able to actually feel the affects of it. Music has definitely been a part of my healing journey. I can now see that moving through the sad songs to the self-empowering songs enabled me to first release the hurt, so that I was able to then embrace the love for myself. The truth is, that song lyrics and the actual music are energy. They both emit a vibration, a frequency that we can feel which can raise our own energy when felt by us. Yes, music has the power to raise our vibration, so for me I felt a little better each time I listened to more positive and empowering songs.

If you also love music, like I do, and would like to make a feel good playlist for yourself, just follow your heart and enlist the songs that either give you strength, open your heart or make you feel good and leave you feeling lighter when you listen to them, sing along with them or dance to them. The following are few of my favourites that rode the waves with me and helped move me from sadness to joy. Each of the songs helped in my healing and my growth, as each one brought me what I needed along the way: to be lifted up, to strengthen my sense of self and to expand my heart. I hope they give you an example of possible types of music to seek out for yourself, so that you can bring healing and love within you too.

- "*I Will Survive*" by Gloria Gaynor was instrumental in the beginning when I was in my rawest moments. Although I was not really sure that I would at the time, I felt the energy of the words, "I WILL" move through me each time I listened or sang it to myself, which in time shifted my beliefs to see the possibilities for a bright future.

- "*Stronger (What Doesn't Kill You)*" by Kelly Clarkson enabled me to build my inner strength. To reaffirm that life's hardships are there to make you stronger. To not leave your power in someone else's hands. I used to listen to it as I walked on the treadmill and found it gave me a rush that at times would bring me to raise my hands in the air as I sang along in my mind and energized me to walk faster. It was truly a Win Win!!

- "*Greatest Love Of All*" by Whitney Houston is a song that I've listened to often in past years and always felt it was a beautiful song. Yet, I felt like I connected to it and the words had a deeper, more profound meaning the more I connected to my higher self. We are all awakening to the love we are and embodying, and integrating that love is a beautiful thing to experience. The first time I sang it out loud with the intention of singing it to myself, I remember feeling each word permeating my body and soul. I was taken over by it and was brought to tears. I realized at that moment that I was beginning to embody the "greatest love of all" and connecting to my higher self. It felt amazingly beautiful! If you are wanting to connect to the love within yourself also, I recommend this song highly.

- "*The Fighter*" by Keith Urban and Carrie Underwood is about the new love in your life who will help you get through the pain of the past and be there for you, pick you up and love you. To me this was an incredible song to sing to myself, as I was both people at the same time, (Carrie and Keith) It felt like my mind was the part asking all the what ifs and doubtful questions and my inner self replied and reaffirmed that I am loved, and that it has my back and will keep me safe and happy always. Each time I sang it with the intention of singing it to myself I felt my own inner power growing within. As each time I was reaffirming to myself that my inner strength (heart and soul) will prevail when my mind(ego) tries to take over. Love, love love this song!!

- "*Close Your Eyes*" by Meghan Trainor is a song that I came across more recently and found the message of showing the world what's beautiful—YOU– to be unbelievably healing. It's a beautiful song about self-love and being your authentic beautiful self. I love it so much that I recommend it to everyone to read the lyrics and sing along to yourself or out loud if you can and notice how you feel. If at first you feel uneasy, that's OK, keep it in your back pocket and do it again in the future when you are feeling like you are not enough and allow it to shift your energy. It's an awesome self-love tool!

I hope these songs inspire you to make your own healing or feel good playlist if you want to. Remember, you give meaning to the words and a song can be sang to yourself, someone else, or the world.

So, whether music is your thing that lifts you up or something else is, embrace whatever it is and engage in it as much as you can. Allow yourself to be who you are. Like I said previously, in the past I would never have told people that I dance or sing to myself when I'm alone in my condo because I used to give others' opinions too much power over me. I would have felt embarrassed about it and probably would've put a negative twist to it in my mind ("I am doing it alone because I am alone and have no one else to dance with"). The thing is, it's not really about anything or anyone else. It's about you and loving yourself enough to give yourself what you need. It's about giving yourself the permission to just do whatever makes your heart sing!

So, what brings you joy? What lifts the darkness into light? It may be music for you too, or it may be something very different. It doesn't really matter what it is, just do you! Take the time to notice how the activities you engage in make you feel and connect to the energy they bring. If it feels good, DO MORE OF IT!!

Chapter 14

Finding Peace

ALLOWING IT IN

Stress, worry and fear are prevalent today and are felt by most of us on a daily basis. In years past, there was not much thought of how these emotions affected us mentally, emotionally or physically, and instead we would unconsciously blame others, our work or even the world events for such feelings. We were unable to or unwilling to take responsibility for our part in creating these feelings in ourselves. But the fact is, stressful things, events and people are a part of our lives. So, how can we co-exist with this and find peace within it all?

Peace is felt within. It is a calmness, an inner knowing that no matter what is happening to us or around us that we are or will be OK. Peace is letting go of control and allowing ourselves and others to be as they are. Peace is trusting ourselves, our journey and the universe. I don't mean to say that we should become doormats or stick our heads in the sand and isolate ourselves away from the world to attain peace. It's quite the opposite, actually. It's being able to live your life as you are, yet no matter what you encounter along the way, you feel the energy of peace within and know the truth that you are indeed separate from it all.

When we long for a change in our inner or outer worlds, we may encounter some blocks or barriers. Our minds may come up with reasons or stories why we can't or shouldn't change, and at times we may choose to give into these thoughts. There may be lifestyle changes needed and perhaps that's not something you find easy to shift, or change. Or you may simply fear others' opinions. And that's all OK! But ask yourself: Who will make YOU a priority if you don't?

We all do many things in our outer worlds to achieve ease and calmness, like soaking in a bubble bath, going to a spa, being creative through painting or sculpting or taking a leisurely walk through nature. As you allow yourself the gift of time to add whatever soothes your soul into your day, know that you are making a subconscious shift. You are telling yourself that you deserve this calmness and you are worthy of it.

I invite you to bring stillness into your day. Even a brief moment will do wonders. Breathe in slowly and deeply, opening your heart a bit more with each inhale, release any tension with each exhale and feel the stress melt away. Notice how your body feels doing this. Also remind yourself daily, or hourly if needed, that you are OK, you are safe and all is well!

Finding peace within, like all growth and healing, is a process that may take time to obtain. Discovering that you want more of it in your life is the first step. Setting an intention and creating it by implementing steps is the next. If your outer world is always busy and filled with drama and chaos it will be more difficult to feel peaceful inside yourself. As the lower energies attached to your life situations will also be felt by you. Setting healthy boundaries, both for yourself and your life, are important aspects on the way to attaining peace. Releasing or choosing to limit time with someone or something that no longer serves you in a positive way can aid in raising your vibration, which in turn then allows a sense of ease within. When you become aware of what you don't want, you begin to see what it is you do want. You will begin to naturally gravitate to the things and people that you want to be around, as they simply feel better. And when your outer world feels more calm and peaceful, you then have space and time to focus on yourself, to connect within, and to consciously choose what you would like to bring into your day.

Also, as you learn to forgive, gain compassion and connect to your higher self, your heart and soul will begin to open. Seeing others with love and accepting them where they are instead of resisting, will also lessen the stress you previously felt. You then can make decisions that are beneficial to the both of you with more ease. Every time you choose to bring a sense of ease into your day, to feel or embody an energy of calmness, your body relaxes, and you simply will begin to feel life is easier somehow.

If you need help finding calmness in your day or would like to take steps to feel more peace within, consider trying some of the following:

- **Become one with nature.** Close your eyes and open your heart to the beauty that surrounds you. Allow yourself to be in the stillness of the moment, and as you open your eyes, gaze around without thought and simply feel your connection to it all. Breathe it all in.

- **Release low energy.** When you notice you're feeling contracted or triggered, feel the energy associated with it and allow it to pass through you. Try not to resist it. Know that it is not really you, but rather a part that has attached itself to you. It may feel like it's real to you in the moment as the negative energy in you feels real and is asking to be released. So, continue to breathe deeply and slowly, let it pass through you and remind yourself of the truth: you are OK!

- **Unplug from technology.** Just be with yourself. Allowing your mind to slow down, even briefly can add a sense of calm to you and your day. There is much to be gained from silence and stillness.

- **Breath work** is essential in connecting within. It calms your mind and allows your heart, mind and body to expand with the energy of love, peace and harmony that is truly you. Integrating this higher energy within often is key. Remember the law of attraction: be the energy you want to attract more of.

- **Listen to or repeat affirmations**, engage in meditation or listen to relaxing music that allows you to feel peaceful and calm.

Here are some affirmations for tranquility:

- I am peace.
- I release all negativity and move into love.
- I have everything I need.
- I am thankful for all that I am and all that I have.
- I am always doing the best I can.

If none of these resonate with you, simply choose something else that does, or create one that feels good to you. There is no right or wrong way to do this.

To begin, just add one thing to your day that creates a sense of calm. Then as it feels right, add other new methods and implement them at different times of the day to see when they suit you best. Be willing to take the time to experience each one fully and become aware of how they make you feel in your mind, body and soul.

Does finding peace within mean you feel this way every minute of every day, and that you live in a bubble of happiness? Not at all. It means you are able to embrace these expansive moments with an open heart. It means that you are able to connect to this feeling and embody the energy of it more often, and when you feel out of alignment (stressed, worried, fearful), you are able to shift back with more ease. Your inner world feels safe and calm, and you literally begin to breathe more easily. Your outer world no longer controls your inner world—you do!

Declutter your outer world and feel more peace in your inner world.

Compassion and Gratitude

We are complex beings and untwisting the tangled webs we've woven within and around us takes time, patience and love. Along the way, it's important that we celebrate each step on our journeys, embrace the now and accept who and where we are in the moment, even if it's not our desired final destination. We must love all aspects of ourselves and allow our hearts and compassion to extend to the person we see in the mirror.

Finding compassion is not something that just happens. It does not come from the mind. It is a feeling inside that enables us to connect deeply with ourselves and others, to understand with our hearts and to feel empathy. To truly feel compassion for others, we must first feel love and compassion for ourselves. For feeling love within opens our hearts, and we are then able to share the love and feel it for others.

I remember doing an online meditation class once and revealing to my teacher how I felt at the time: sad, alone and unloved. I was the only student as it was a private class, so it felt safe and my feelings flowed out easily. It was definitely a low point in my journey, and I remember I was quite emotional, with tears continually flowing down my cheeks as I spoke. A few days later as I was thinking about the class, I remembered that it had been recorded and honestly, at first had no interest in watching it, as seeing myself on camera felt very uncomfortable to me. Yet the thought to watch kept entering my mind. So, a few days later I sat down, opened my laptop and began watching the session unfold. I was taken by surprise when I arrived at the moment where I began to get emotional. As I witnessed myself crying, it was as if I was staring at someone else and I felt my heart ache for her. My stomach began to sink and a lump formed in my throat as I tried to push down the emotion that was rising within me, but in the next moment I found myself crying too. I had an uncontrollable urge to hug the woman on the screen—ME! It may sound weird to some, but I just began talking to her. I told her she was beautiful, worthy and lovable. It was quite a liberating moment for me, and it has shifted how I connect with myself ever since. In fact, in future moments of sadness, I have often looked in the mirror to show myself the compassion I needed. When you look directly into your own eyes, I believe you can reach your soul, and this is an incredibly powerful thing.

In the moments when we are feeling down and out, it can seem almost impossible to feel grateful. Things may be extremely difficult to navigate as low energy encompasses us, leaving us feeling stuck. Yet, this is exactly the time when finding the smallest thing to be grateful for can shift our negative thoughts and energies to more positive ones. By doing this, we allow a conscious shift to begin in us. It raises our vibration and we feel different and therefore see differently. One moment of gratitude has the potential to grow into more. Each time we shift, we then naturally begin to gravitate towards these higher energies and feelings.

Keeping a gratitude journal or simply saying two or three things you are grateful for every morning or evening can slowly alter how you see things and how you feel. Find gratitude for the everyday things: your home, the air you breathe, the warmth of the sun, a beautiful plant or flower. When you live with an open heart, you are able to feel the loving energy from everything around you and within you, and in turn, that energy will flow outwardly from you. Remember, we are connected to the energy of all things. Feeling gratitude for the many blessings you have in your life allows you to feel abundant and fulfilled in the present, thus relinquishing you from a past mindset of lack. When you truly feel gratitude, love and compassion within, you are aligned with the higher energy these feelings bring. Who you truly are shines through more easily and more often, bringing more peace and contentment with it.

Chapter 15

A Destination with No End

"BE" IN EACH DAY

We all want to create our best lives, to feel connected and loved, to belong to something and to have a sense of purpose. Yet, many of us are living our days unaware that we already have the potential for all of that within us, and that each step we take to grow, learn and evolve brings us closer to those goals. Life is a continual journey with no real ending. Each step along the way is meant to be embraced. We are not here to have perfect or easy lives. We are here to evolve, to learn and grow our minds, hearts, bodies and souls. If we can allow ourselves to connect with and feel our own energies, understand our own minds and see our own perceived difficulties as lessons or opportunities for growth, we will then be able to shift into a more conscious state of being. From there, we can create more of what we desire. Learning to "be" in each day means accepting who and where you are and finding gratitude for where it is you find yourself. Releasing the past, old beliefs and patterns is imperative to attaining this. Living in the present moment and clearing the mind clutter is also key.

Beginning to learn how to do these things can feel overwhelming if you are in a difficult place. If you find you are at a place in your life where you feel stuck or lost, perhaps one of the following questions might help to move you forward:

- Can you allow yourself the gift of time needed to begin self-healing? If not, why is that?

- Who do you see in the mirror? Can you accept and love who you see in this moment?

- Can you see the beauty that surrounds you?

- Can you see that there are many roads that lead to where you desire to be? If so, can you allow certain doors to close, and are you willing to walk through any new ones that open?

Be gentle with yourself while asking these questions. If you feel uneasy or an uncomfortable feeling arising within you, that's OK. In fact, it's actually a good thing. It's a sign that you need to pause, accept where you are in the moment and ask yourself, "Why do I feel this way?" Allow yourself to be how you are and who you are. Simply start the conversation with yourself. From there, notice how you feel as the answers arise. Self-discovery leads to self-awareness, which is key to growth and healing.

You cannot change who you are, without seeing who you were.

Remember, we are all here to grow and evolve, and we all will achieve this in the manner that is right for us and at a time when we are ready. Every aspect of yourself or your life that you shine the light of consciousness on, accept and choose to heal, embrace, forgive or release leads you down your path. And the more authentic you show up, the more you will allow yourself to just "be" you.

When you are able to show up as your true self and be that person in your life, you will become a light for others. Your heart will expand and your passion will grow. So, if you find yourself struggling now, know it doesn't have to be there forever. Simply be willing to discover, embrace and love the real you.

A few questions for inspiration:

- What will you imprint on the world?

- Who are you REALLY? Are you willing to let your true self shine through?

- If you could do what your heart desires right now, what would that be?

Remember, there are limitless possibilities in you, for you and in your life.

Knowing the Truth

I am an energetic, beautiful spiritual human being. I am now able to see with ease and clarity who I was and why. I can also see the level of conscious awareness I had been carrying with me throughout the stages of my life and the lessons and growth I needed to help raise my vibration in order to move into the future with more courage, love and awareness.

In the past, my level of awareness or consciousness was not always understood or embraced by others, as my thoughts did not always align with theirs. As a result, I believe that I have always been unconsciously fighting to be me, and yet ironically I did not yet know who I truly was.

Having my life turned upside down was truly the most traumatic and painful thing in my life, and yet, it turned out to be what led me to the biggest blessings in my life!

I love me! I am perfectly imperfect and that's OK! I have my light and it is me! The heart, compassion and love that has always been a part of me is now shining brightly, effortlessly and for most part, authentically. I have released, let go and forgiven what I needed to, and I will continue to do this as best I can as life continues. If I feel frustrated, stressed or anxious, I know those feelings are there to show me that I'm out of alignment with my true self. They are not there to defend, justify or judge myself or others. I listen, feel and hear my mind and body as best I can in any given moment, and I am also willing to find acceptance in what is. I have always had a big heart, the gift of gab and a love for people, which were and still are my strongest attributes, I believe. Without them, this book would not have become a reality.

We are one! The more we love ourselves and raise our energy and consciousness, the more it will flow outwards to hopefully become the dominant vibration within us, around us and in the world.

Simply… *Be the vibration you wish to attract more of and to you.*

The following are a few gentle reminders to take with you as you move forward on your path:

- Love who you are, not who you think you should be.

- See others with kindness and compassion—they are you in different shoes!

- You only know who someone is by who they show you they are. You are not responsible for the aspects of themselves that they keep hidden.

- We are meant to travel our own paths. When you need to part with someone, it may simply mean that you have grown as much as you can together and are meant to move forward without them. Your intentions or energies may no longer be aligned, and even though you aren't aware of it, the universe is!

- Find joy and love in all that you are and all that you do.

- Taking steps to heal and grow are a personal and intimate way to connect with and love yourself. It allows all of you to shine through.

- Try to remember sometimes unanswered prayers are gifts from the universe. When I found myself heartbroken, all I could do was wish for my life to go back to what it was. Yet, what I ultimately became aware of was that what I really missed was more the idea of what my life used to be. It was what I thought I needed to be whole. The universe does not always give us what we think we need or want, and even though it doesn't feel good at the time, it's ultimately for our higher good.

- Check in with yourself daily; listen to your mind, body and soul, and always give yourself what you need.

- *Trust in, believe in, and embrace the journey! It truly is MIRACULOUS!!*

Lost Now Found

Throughout my journey, I have learned, practised and integrated the new, and I have accepted, released and forgiven the old. I have grown back into who I've always been, yet, forgot I was.

The perfect way to end my book is with music, so I'd like to share two songs that to me summarize my journey from heartache to awakening my heart, mind, body and soul. The first, is a song that I came across one day and was the epiphany of my journey: who I was and who I grew into. To me, it's my declaration of ultimately finding myself and loving who I am! The second is a song that has travelled with me throughout the years and I have loved always, yet now also holds a new, more deeper meaning to me.

Alicia Keys is an artist that I've always connected with. To me, she embodies a sense of realness in her music and in herself. One day after several years of healing, I came across a song of hers that I had not heard before, yet one that I truly believe on some level was written for me.

The name: "Brand New Me."

I sobbed the first time I heard it. I felt the truth of each word in my soul and felt the energy of them move within me and into my heart. The words of the song felt tailored to me, my life and how I now saw myself. As we grow, we change. We begin to show ourselves more love, we make ourselves a priority or at the very least we become part of the equation. We begin to see ourselves as *somebody* and allow ourselves to be seen and heard. Sometimes, others can take offence to our growth, and make it into a "bad" thing because we've changed. Perhaps, in their eyes, they can only see how the "changed you" now affects them. I love this song, because for me I felt like I was shouting out to the world, that "Yes, I am brand new, and it's OK!" I found this song at the perfect time, when I could feel each word as my truth. Finding it at the perfect time was not surprising to me, as divine timing is always at play. Yet, I still feel in awe each time I notice it, and I was so thankful for it! It became my song to me and I would sing it out loud, often looking at myself in the mirror as I sang. Empowerment does not even describe the inner feelings I had. I felt each word, meant each word and believed each word. It is indeed what showed me without a doubt, that I have found myself.

Thank you, Alicia!

The second song is "The Dance" by Garth Brooks. For many years, this song has been a part of my life. In the past

I've always thought of it as a romantic song, and I guess I still do. Yet, it wasn't until the last few years with my life changing that I now also see a deeper meaning in it.

The words of this song, to me, say it all perfectly. They illustrate how I see life now. No one really knows where our lives will lead us, and yes there may be times when we're better off not knowing what's ahead. Throughout the dance we call life we will live, love, learn and we will grow with the people on our journey. And it is *all* of these steps that we take together, how we grow with them or perhaps because of them, that is to be cherished as we move forward, not the pain. If we are fully living our life, we will undoubtedly experience it all, both joy and pain. There are always hills and valleys. The truth is though, if we never new pain, we would not be able to feel joy.

I encourage you to look at and embrace the whole dance: each step and each experience with an open heart. If you can, you will begin to feel gratitude for your whole journey, including the pain, as you will be able to see the "good," that came from the perceived "bad". You will be consciously aware, and therefore you will know in your heart that every difficulty or moment of darkness is leading you to a lighter, more peaceful and joyful future on your road to becoming more authentically you!

For me, I wouldn't have missed the dance!!

Thank you, Garth!

From My Heart to Yours, I wish you love, peace and joy and I hope this book is a small part in you achieving that!!

WORKS CITED

Brooks, Garth, "The Dance", *Garth Brooks*, Capitol Nashville, 1989.

Brown, Brene, *The Gifts of Imperfection*, Hazelden Publishing, Simon & Schuster, 2010.

Clarkson, Kelly, "Stronger, What Doesn't Kill You", *Stronger*, RCA, 2011.

Gaynor, Gloria, "I Will Survive", *Love Tracks*, Polydor, 1978 (written by Freddie Perren, Dino Fekaris).

Houston, Whitney, "Greatest Love Of All", *The Greatest Soundtrack*, Arista, 1977.

Keys, Alicia, "Brand New Me", *Girl On Fire*, RCA Records, Sony Music Entertainment, 2012.

Parenthood, "I'm Cooler Than You Think", Season 2, Episode 3, Sept 28, 2010 (with Dax Shepherd, Tina Lifford, Tyree Brown, Joy Bryant).

Tolle, Eckhart, *The Power Of Now*, New World Library, 1999.

Tolle, Eckhart, *A New Earth*, Viking Press, Dutton, 2005.

Trainor, Meghan, "Close Your Eyes", *Title*, Epic Records, 2015.

Urban, Keith (Carrie Underwood), "The Fighter", *Ripcord*, Capitol Records, 2016.

Printed in Canada